RUBY STAR WRAPPING

FIG. 5
FIG. 7
FIG. 9
One-room, kitchenette apartment created from a
income, and a profitable investment for the
plete with every needed facility, all
FIG. 10

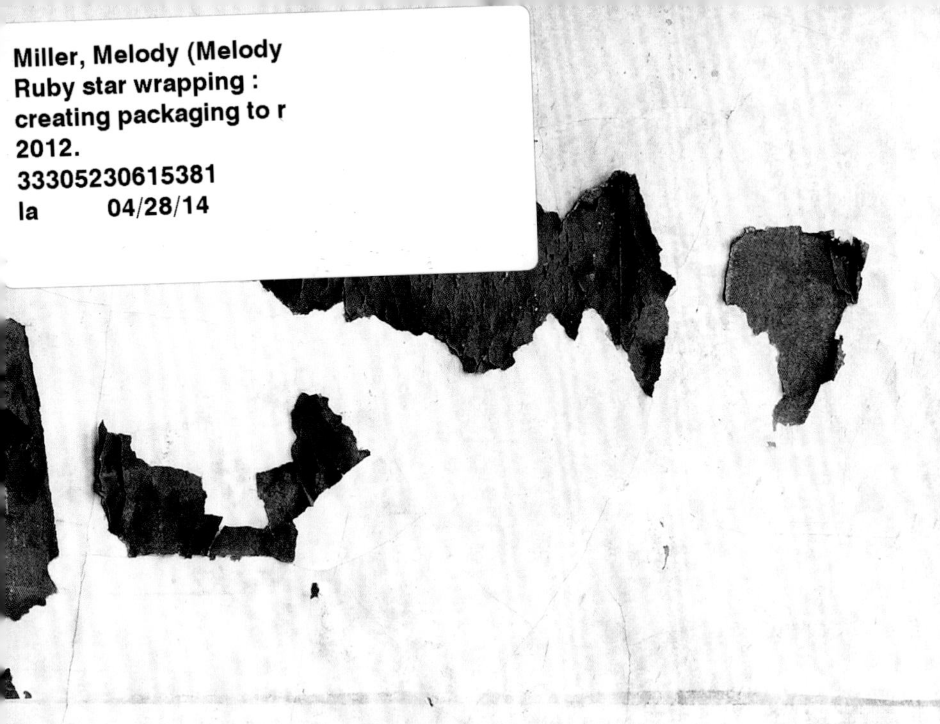

RUBY STAR WRAPPING

Creating Packaging to Reuse, Regive, and Relove

MELODY MILLER & ALLISON TANNERY

Boston & London
2012

Roost Books
An imprint of Shambhala Publications, Inc.
Horticultural Hall
300 Massachusetts Avenue
Boston, Massachusetts 02115
roostbooks.com

9 8 7 6 5 4 3 2 1

First Edition
Printed in China

♾ This edition is printed on acid-free paper that meets the American National Standards Institute Z39.48 Standard.

♻ Shambhala Publications makes every effort to print on recycled paper. For more information please visit www.shambhala.com.

Distributed in the United States by Random House, Inc., and in Canada by Random House of Canada Ltd.

Designed by
Blake C. Tannery

Library of Congress Cataloging-in-Publication Data

Miller, Melody (Melody Brown)
Ruby star wrapping: creating packaging to reuse, regive, and relove
Melody Miller and Allison Tannery.—First edition.
Pages cm
ISBN 978-1-59030-999-5 (pbk.: alk. paper) 1. Handicraft. 2. Gift wrapping. 3. Scrap materials.
I. Tannery, Allison. II. Title.
TT857.M55 2012
745.54—dc23
2011051737

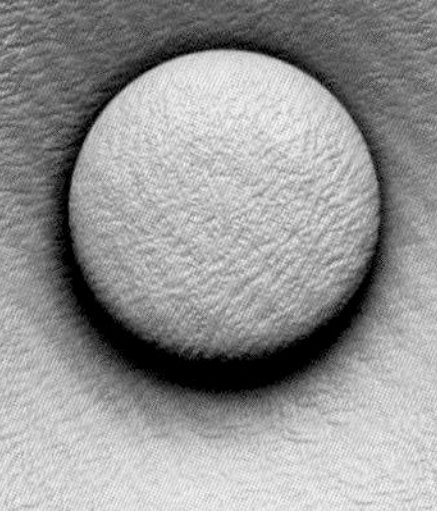

from allison

My son told me no one reads these things. But I've dreamed of my first dedication for forever, so this will be the most needlessly wordy dedication possible in all craft book history.

Melody, you are a real friend: generous, supportive, and a crazy creative business partner. You told me I could do this. My family, I adore you, but the first dedication goes to Melody. Without her, I'd have no book to write. From the bottom of my house Chardonnay–soaked heart, thank you, Melody.

Blake? You know everything I could say here, so since our editor rightly told me I was just too wordy, remember this. From the first margarita, I knew you'd get the life vest.

Jake, Kat, Blue, and Hart? What can I say. You didn't help *that* much. But I love you all, and *appreciate* the challenge of writing an entire book in four months while being your full-time mother. You would all get the next life vest. Promise.

And last, but not at all least, to Slameron, who let me run away when I needed, and who kept the door open.

from melody

To creativity, to imagination, to the loveliness and messiness that is life itself. And to my beautiful friend, Allison, for being along for the ride. Greg, you're my hero. And my sweet Iliana and Finn, you make it all worthwhile.

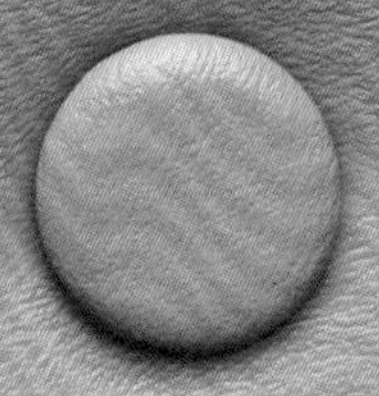

MAY NO GIFT BE TOO SMALL TO GIVE,
NOR TOO SIMPLE TO RECEIVE, WHICH IS WRAPPED
IN THOUGHTFULNESS, AND TIED WITH LOVE.

L. O. BAIRD

CONTENTS

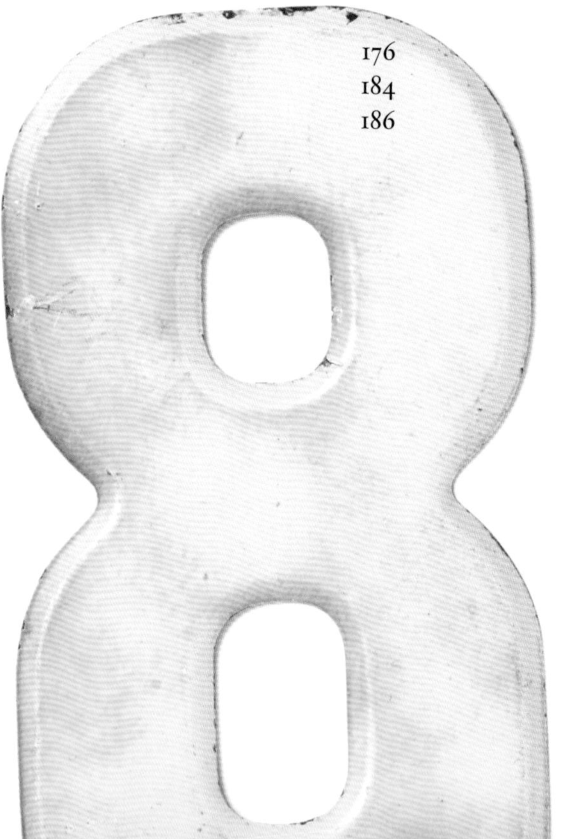

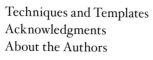

FOREWORD

Someone recently asked me if *Sew, Mama, Sew!*, my website and blog on fabric and sewing, had a "tipping point"—an event or time we could identify when we went from relatively unknown to fairly well-recognized in the online sewing community. I absolutely knew the answer to be November of 2007 when we hosted our first Handmade Holidays event, posting several tutorials for gifts to sew every day of the month. For thirty days we watched our traffic grow and we were continually delighted to read the comments from thankful fans who were inspired to make their own holiday gifts. We learned something about our readers and customers that month that continues to guide us to this day—this is a community that loves to *give*, and if we can give something we've made with our own two hands then all the better. We make Christmas gifts and wedding gifts and shower gifts. We make for our children, our parents, and our hard-to-shop-for fathers-in-law. We make for girlfriends, boyfriends, and online friends. We make for children in orphanages, families in crisis, and seniors in need. It's wonderful to be part of such a generous community.

Despite all the making and giving going on, it's surprisingly rare that we come across blog posts that detail the ways in which sewists and other crafters present their handmade gifts to the recipient. Certainly baker's twine and washi tape have had their day in the sun, but beyond talking about these little package adornments, people are relatively quiet about how they wrap their presents. That's why I was so excited to hear about Melody and Allison's book. I am a huge fan of Melody's fabric lines and her vintage-yet-modern style, and I love anything she makes.

While I knew Melody and Allison would bring great style to gift wrapping, another reason I took such a great interest in *Ruby Star Wrapping* is the earth-friendly benefits of packaging with reusable, recyclable, and/or repurposed items. In December 2010, *Sew, Mama, Sew!* collaborated with the *Green Bag Lady* to host The Green Grocery Bag Challenge, a call-to-action in which we encouraged sewists to wrap their holiday gifts in cloth bags that could later be used by the recipients as grocery bags. In the process of promoting that event, I learned that United States consumers generate four million tons of wrapping paper and shopping bag waste during the December holiday season alone—a statistic that should give us all pause next time we reach for a roll of gift wrap. Since then I've been committed to giving all my gifts in reusable packages, and I'm slowly but surely encouraging family, friends, and our blog readers to do the same. A book like this is a great resource that can help us all make greener choices when it comes to wrapping.

I truly believe that the presentation of handmade gifts should be as thoughtful and artful as the gift itself, and if we can help the earth in the process, then we've added meaning to what we do. This book, full of wrapping suggestions from two talented people, is sure to inspire you to be as creative and conscientious about packaging your gifts as you are about making them.

Happy sewing and wrapping,

KRISTIN LINK
Sew, Mama, Sew!

INTRODUCTION: THE READ ME FIRST

INT. LIVING ROOM - 6:22 AM CMAS DAY

Four pairs of small feet rush to the brightly lit tree. They see beneath it mounds of festively wrapped gifts in colorfully coordinated papers and shiny stick-on bows. They gasp. Bask in the reflective glow. So. Many. Presents.

INT. LIVING ROOM - 6:41 AM CMAS DAY

Bleary eyed, Mother and Father enter. They cannot find the tree, any of the unwrapped gifts, or the children. They assume their respective Christmas morning duties, and begin the dig out and clean up.

EXT. BOTTOM OF DRIVEWAY, BY CURB - 4:06 PM CMAS DAY

Eight lawn-sized trash bags of cardboard, wrapping, ribbon, tissue paper, used tape, one new Hotwheels, and Dad's holiday slippers sit awaiting Monday morning pickup. Just *what* happened to those slippers will remain a point of family mystery for years to come.

The Christmases of my childhood are much like this scene—magical mounds of carefully coordinated sparkly packages, our eager fingers ripping through the bows and paper, flinging tissue through the air as we tore, cut, and clawed our way to the goodies inside the gift wrapping. After the first awe-inspiring glance, we hardly even *saw* what wrapped our presents. Was that year multicolored plaid with red velvet? Green foil and silver curly ribbon? Butcher paper and hundreds of hot glued Hershey's Kisses? (All of this after my poor Mother had spent many days and dollars in the planning and preparing.) After all the wrapping, ripping, and tossing aside, we certainly never gave thought to saving all that paper, ribbon, and tissue. I mean, that would require painstaking care: little scissors to slice through the tape, neatly folding crumpled paper, organizing and storing, and a lot of time. We'd be our grandmothers before we were twenty! (I'm sorry, Grandma Boo. I understand you and your little pocket scissors now.) Weeks of preparation went out the curb in less than forty-five minutes.

Now that we are in an era that is becoming increasingly focused on sustainable living, all the buying and trashing feel antiquated—like trying to keep the Pony Express running in the age of email and video conferencing. It costs an awful lot of money, natural resources, and manpower to keep all those riders and horses happy! And because any cause's BFF is a good statistic—as a good statistic will prove anything you want proven—we dug this up: according to the Sierra Club, if every American family wrapped *just three gifts* this year in something that could be reused, we would save enough paper to fill 45,000 football fields. When so many of the problems that surround us feel depressingly insurmountable, this is something we can do. I will not single-handedly end world hunger, but by putting just a little more thought into how we wrap our gifts, we can help to lessen the amount of waste we produce.

While we can feel all warm and fuzzy about the environmental benefits, what really makes us happy about the projects in this book is that they remind us of the often unrealized potential in the act of giving a gift. When wrapped with thought, beauty, and a little ingenuity, the gift package can be a gift in itself. In a place like Japan, the gift has always started with the very presentation. You wrap a gift to show your sincerity, originality, and creativity—to honor the one you are gifting even beyond the gift itself. In this way, the object given *and* the wrapping work in tandem to create a whole—a delightful *experience*. It's a twist on the rip and toss, and we like it.

In his amazing book, *How to Wrap Five Eggs*, Hideyuki Oka uses gorgeous photography and thought-provoking words to tell the story of the earliest Japanese packaging. This packaging was accomplished by wrapping an object in whatever materials lay at hand, which included leaves, bamboo, straw, clay, and other natural materials. He expresses the sense of "delight in the look and feel of ordinary, humble things." While we appreciate the ordinary and humble, we really like the idea of using the materials around us. Those materials might not be *momiji* (Japanese maple) leaves but rather scraps of pretty fabrics, food packaging, newspaper, craft supplies, and the miraculous hot glue gun. (Isn't a glue gun in everyone's modern natural setting?) What we want to share with the Japanese is this simple philosophy: a unique, charming presentation can be made from even the most unassuming objects.

In another wonderful gift-wrapping idea, the Japanese also use *origata*: intricately folded paper used to only partly conceal the gift inside, giving the recipient a little tease and a promise of the gift to come. The folds communicated ideas such as "good luck," "be happy," or "That's so sad. I'm sorry." Apparently, there is an *entire* language of pretty little folds that whisper messages to the recipient. We can't show you how to say "I'm pregnant!" in folded *National Geographic* pages, but we can show you how to infuse your gift wrapping with personality and emotion. We think nearly nothing says "I care" like a dish of piping hot cheese grits in an adorable quilted cover, all tied up with a big bow. Your gift will be lovely, tasty, aromatic, and super-easy to reuse. (Well, the grits can't be reused, but the quilted cover can be.)

From the simple materials to the thoughtful sentiments, the projects in *Ruby Star Wrapping* are greater than the sum of their parts. They are artful, charming, and sincere. With all the ingenuity, care, and

personal zing going into these packages, they certainly shouldn't be thrown out with the regular ol' wrapping, right? Right! That's why these wrappings are designed to live a second or third life—to wrap another gift or to be used somewhere in the home. Some will even live a life longer than the gift itself (that bottle of wine may not last the night, definitely won't in *my* house, but the adorable fabric wrap in which it was given makes a great tea towel that can be used over and over). Take a page from Japanese culture: *everything* can be made beautiful, and every gift can be wrapped in honesty and authenticity. Remember this, and then add some basic creative skills, and you will equal ready to go.

Preparation: The Read Me Next

OK. So you're all prepped to make awesome, thoughtful, beautiful, and resourceful gift wrapping? Here's where we give you the tips, skillful techniques, essential tools, and *Ruby Star Wrapping* insider secrets to go from drug store paper to endless options in memorable packaging. We're drawing from not only ancient tradition but future forward thinking. Why do you want to do this? Because it's cool! Be one of the cool kids! In truth, it really is lovely, economical, and environmentally friendly.

To get into the ideas behind *Ruby Star Wrapping,* you'll want to start collecting fabric scraps, buttons, vintage linens, sheets or pillow cases, ribbon, Japanese washi tape, pretty papers, and any other thing that catches your eye and makes you think *oooooooohhhh.* We've been at notions shops, especially those in the Fashion District in New York City, and nearly come undone with all the gorgeous possibilities. (OK. So we're easily entertained.) It can occasionally feel awkward to justify twenty-nine dollars in ribbons you don't know how to use yet, but then they'll be there just when you're in need. (At least, Melody insists this is so, and lo and behold, I've learned it to be true. After our idiot dog ate the straps off a bag Mel made for me, I had beautiful ribbon to replace them!) You can also save shells, twine, rope, and pieces of wrapping salvaged from other gifts you've received—just like Grandma used to.

Melody collects fabric scraps, and I hoard sturdy boxes. She loves stickers and interesting papers, and I love cigar boxes and my hot glue gun. Together we have learned this: combining interesting paper or fabric with buttons, trim, ribbon, and nearly anything else you find nifty creates amazing packaging. An old bed sheet can make dozens of 5-Minute Party Pouches, and a washed and prettied-up pasta sauce jar can hold those odd rubber bracelets shaped like animals and musical instruments that your niece desperately wants.

Many, though not all, of these projects are sewn. Basic supplies to have on hand include sharp scissors (Melody says a pair for paper, and another for fabric, and never the twain shall meet), pinking shears, cutting mats, a straight

edge, threads (we like Gutterman best for their gorgeous colors), and a sewing machine. Have some pins, a few needles, and as intimated previously, the hot glue gun (my best friend). Although I hate them, an iron is pretty necessary, and if you don't like starch, a spray bottle of water is practically as good. Several projects call for a product like Stitch Witchery, Wonder Under, or pillow stuffing, and a few require fabric glue, spray adhesive, or craft glue. There are times when a rotary cutter is much easier to use than scissors, and a quilter's clear grid ruler can be immensely helpful in cutting fabrics neatly and keeping corners square.

Beyond the ordinary craft tools, keep your eye out for common materials that can be given a new life. We recycle household items like cereal and granola bar boxes, oatmeal canisters, and tin cans; good jars from pickles, sauces, and cheese dip; lovely bottles from root beer, sodas, or rum; tired tea towels, a lonely pillowcase that lost its mate; T-shirts and button-downs no longer worn or that might be stained but are still good in the right places.

Where the accessories are concerned, a few would be great to just have on hand. If you had a few hours one day to get a bunch of ribbon made, rolled, and stored, then when gift-giving time comes, that is already good to go. The gift garlands can be considered in the same way, and depending on the storage space you have, some of the projects could be at least partially assembled and stored away until needed. If you can figure out a way to plan and prepare ahead, go for it. It'll make the entire experience even more accessible.

From our instructions, use what you wish and improvise for fun or necessity. Some of us might need very specific instructions. (Ahem, that would be me, Allison. For instance, I didn't know that when you see measurements, they are always read as width by height. So although Melody said it is probably not necessary, I'm telling you, when you see measurements, it is *width × height.*) Some of us (like Melody) only need a bit of direction and we're off. Consider the ideas in this book to be the launching pad you may need, or the minute details you can't live without.

Our point is this: have fun and create packaging that can be reused in an endless number of ways. Think outside the gift box. We're including tips, suggestions, and a little inspiration for how your project can be reused. The friends who receive these wonderful packages will be inspired. It'll be like that old camp song, "It Only Takes a Spark." You don't know that one? "It only takes a spark, to get the fire going. . . ." Still no? "And soon all those around, will warm up in its glowing." Huh. Just me. Anyway, once your friends see the possibilities, they too will want to get into gift packaging to reuse, regive, and relove, passing on the idea of recycling with charm and creativity. Go. Make something good.

THINGS ARE NOT DIFFICULT TO MAKE. WHAT IS DIFFICULT IS PUTTING OURSELVES IN A STATE OF MIND TO MAKE THEM.
✿ CONSTANTIN BRANCUSI ✿

FEDERAL RESERVE NOTE
THIS NOTE IS LEGAL TENDER
FOR ALL DEBTS, PUBLIC AND PRIVATE
TWO DOLLARS
E41480548A
WASHINGTON, D.C.
SERIES 1976
THE UNITED STATES OF AMERICA
TWO DOLLARS
50

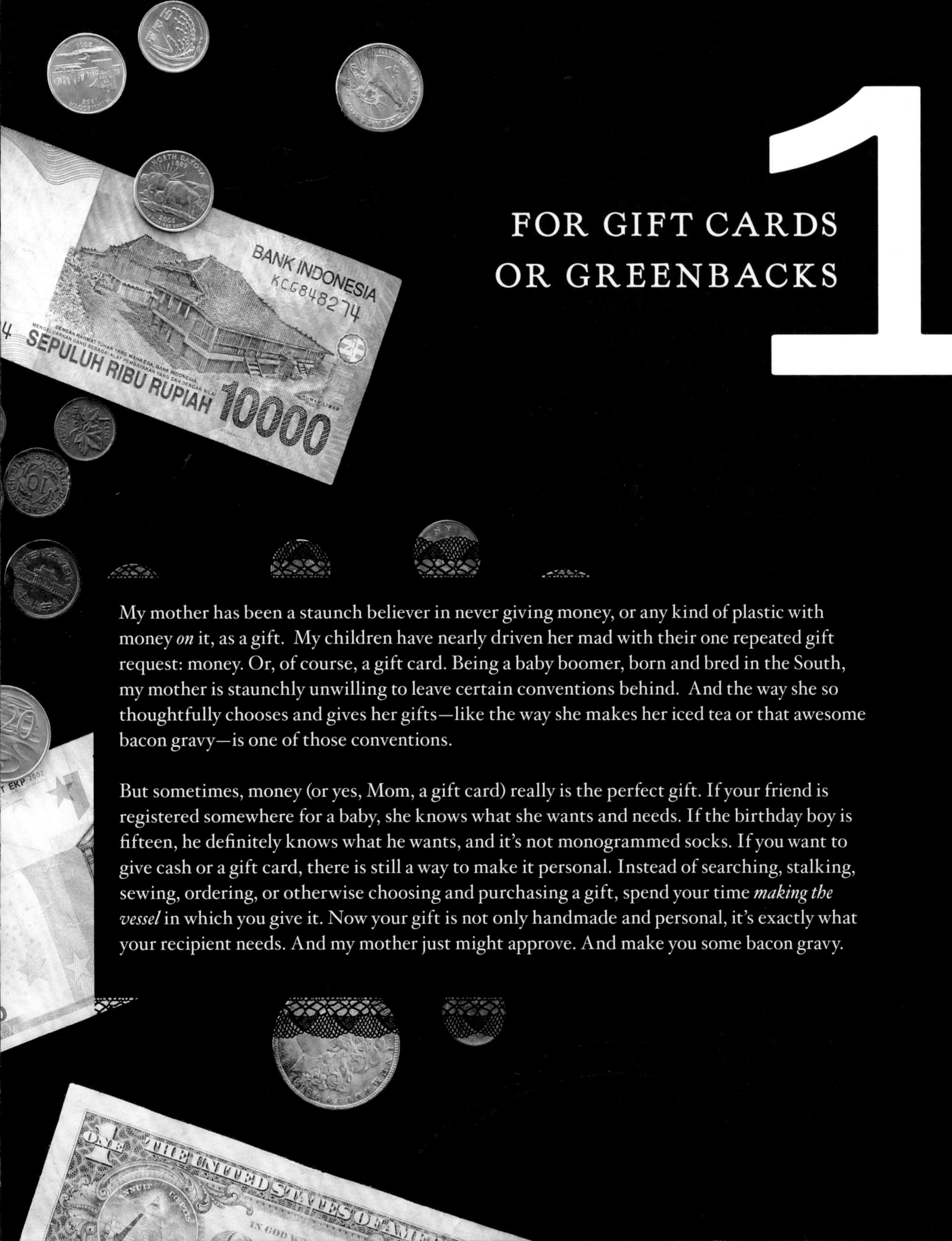

1 FOR GIFT CARDS OR GREENBACKS

My mother has been a staunch believer in never giving money, or any kind of plastic with money *on* it, as a gift. My children have nearly driven her mad with their one repeated gift request: money. Or, of course, a gift card. Being a baby boomer, born and bred in the South, my mother is staunchly unwilling to leave certain conventions behind. And the way she so thoughtfully chooses and gives her gifts—like the way she makes her iced tea or that awesome bacon gravy—is one of those conventions.

But sometimes, money (or yes, Mom, a gift card) really is the perfect gift. If your friend is registered somewhere for a baby, she knows what she wants and needs. If the birthday boy is fifteen, he definitely knows what he wants, and it's not monogrammed socks. If you want to give cash or a gift card, there is still a way to make it personal. Instead of searching, stalking, sewing, ordering, or otherwise choosing and purchasing a gift, spend your time *making the vessel* in which you give it. Now your gift is not only handmade and personal, it's exactly what your recipient needs. And my mother just might approve. And make you some bacon gravy.

GIFT CARD ELEPHANT SOFTIE

These petite pillows just might be our company mascot. They are one of the very first things that Melody ever sewed, and *the* very first thing that started to really sell. When Melody and I first put our heads together on her cutie cushions, we both wanted to market their adorableness, but I suggested adding a pocket for little lost teeth. (She'd never heard of a tooth fairy pillow, whaaaa?) The day Melody put the tooth cushions in her etsy shop, she got a call from *Daily Candy*, who wanted to feature them right away. They went on to catch the attention of people and places like *Design Mom, ohdeedoh,* and *Cool Mom Picks*. We were both so excited to see something actually catch a little fire! While we've moved on to other endeavors, and dream of many more, we just can't leave the elephant behind. We love the elephant.

Have

- This is mostly a scrap fabric project. You need two pieces of fabric no smaller than 17" × 11". These can be solid pieces, or patchwork.
- Smaller scraps for the pocket: two pieces at least 5½" × 3½" from which to cut the flap, and a piece at least 6" × 6" from which to cut the pocket
- Stuffing (We use Fairfield Poly-Fil.)
- Straight pins
- Elephant Softie patterns (page 178)

OPTIONAL, BUT HELPFUL

- Buttons: two that are between ⅜" and ½" for eyes, one larger button for pocket
- Velcro, if you don't like sewing buttonholes
- Spray starch
- Rotary cutter or craft knife
- Cutting mat
- Straight edge

Prepare

1. Photocopy or print the paper pattern pieces. First prepare the elephant template. Carefully cut away and discard the elephant shape, but keep the page that you cut it from. (If you photocopy the pattern from the book, also cut out the surrounding rectangle as indicated; if you print from the PDF, cut off the side of the page, as indicated.) The pattern piece should measure 13" × 11" and will have elephant-shaped hole cut out. This will be your elephant pattern. Cut the pocket pieces and discard the flap portion, according to the instructions on the pattern.

2. Trace the outside of the rectangle (*not* the elephant) onto your front and back fabrics, and cut both fabrics to the exact size of the rectangle.
   TIP: To cut more quickly, stack the two fabrics with the pattern piece on top and use a rotary cutter and straight edge to cut both fabrics at once.

3. Trace, and cut out the pocket piece from fabric.
   TIP: Use pinking shears to help avoid fraying, or serge or zigzag stitch the edges.

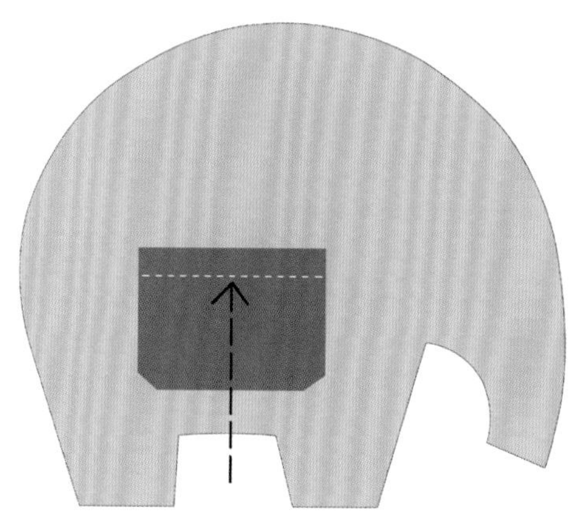

FIG. A1

MAKE

THE POCKET

The pocket flap here is optional. If you don't want a pocket flap, only follow steps 3, 4, 5, and 12. Then, move directly to the next section, The Elephant.

1. For the pocket flap, use two pieces of fabric that are at least 5½" × 3½". Place them right sides together, and trace the inside shape of the pocket flap onto the center of the stacked fabric. Mark a few Xs on the top line you just traced (where you see the Xs on the pattern piece). Pin once in the center. Sew along your traced line. *Do not* sew the top line, with the row of Xs. Cut directly across the top line (with the Xs), and approximately ¼" outside your sewn lines. Flip the sewn piece inside out. Use a chopstick or knitting needle to push out the corners. Iron the pocket flap flat.

2. Sew (and cut) a buttonhole in the center of the pocket flap, about ½" from the bottom edge. The buttonhole should be slightly wider than the button.

TIP: Are you buttonhole challenged? Try sewing on a patch of Velcro instead. You can still stitch a pretty button to the front of the flap. It will be our little secret.

3. Find the pocket piece that you cut out. Place the pocket on your ironing board, right side down. Mist it with spray starch. Beginning with the two bottom diagonal corners, fold and iron the fabric back diagonally by ½". Then fold and iron the bottom edge and the two side edges back by ½". Finally, fold the top edge down 1", twice. Using a ¾" seam allowance, stitch once across the front top of the pocket to hold this fold down.

4. Lay the fabric for the back of the elephant (the pocket side) right side up on a flat surface. Place the elephant template piece face down on top (so the trunk is pointed to the right), and align all edges.

5. Place the pocket right side up on this fabric. Center with the section between the two elephant legs, and raised about 1" toward the center of the elephant (figure A1).

FIG. A2

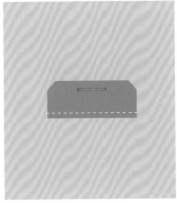

FIG. A3

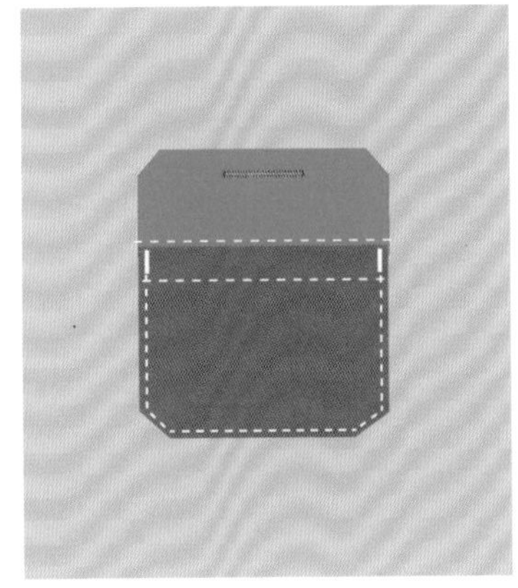

FIG. A4

6. Lightly draw a pencil line on the elephant fabric, to mark the placement of the top of the pocket, from its left edge to the right. Put the pocket and your template aside.

7. Place the pocket flap on top of the elephant fabric, so the top (unstitched) edge meets the line you just drew. The front of the flap will be face up (figure A2).

8. Sew a straight line across the top of the flap, approximately ¼" below the top edge.

9. Trim the top edge of the flap as close as you can to your new stitch (aim for approximately ⅛").

10. Flip the pocket flap all the way up (make sure all the fabric underneath remains flat, especially the large elephant piece), and sew a straight line across the flap ¼" from the bottom edge (figure A3). This stitched line will hide the ragged edge.

11. Place the pocket face up on the elephant fabric. The pocket should just cover up the bottom edge of the flap (figure A4).

12. Sew the pocket to the elephant fabric, as close to the edge as possible (approximately ⅛" or less). Be sure to backstitch several times at the top two corners of the pocket, as the stitches will come undone over time if they are not reinforced. (Don't sew across the pocket top!)

13. Fold the flap back down, and use a pencil to mark a dot through the center of the buttonhole onto the pocket itself. This dot will show you where your button should go.

14. Use a needle and thread to sew the button to the pocket.

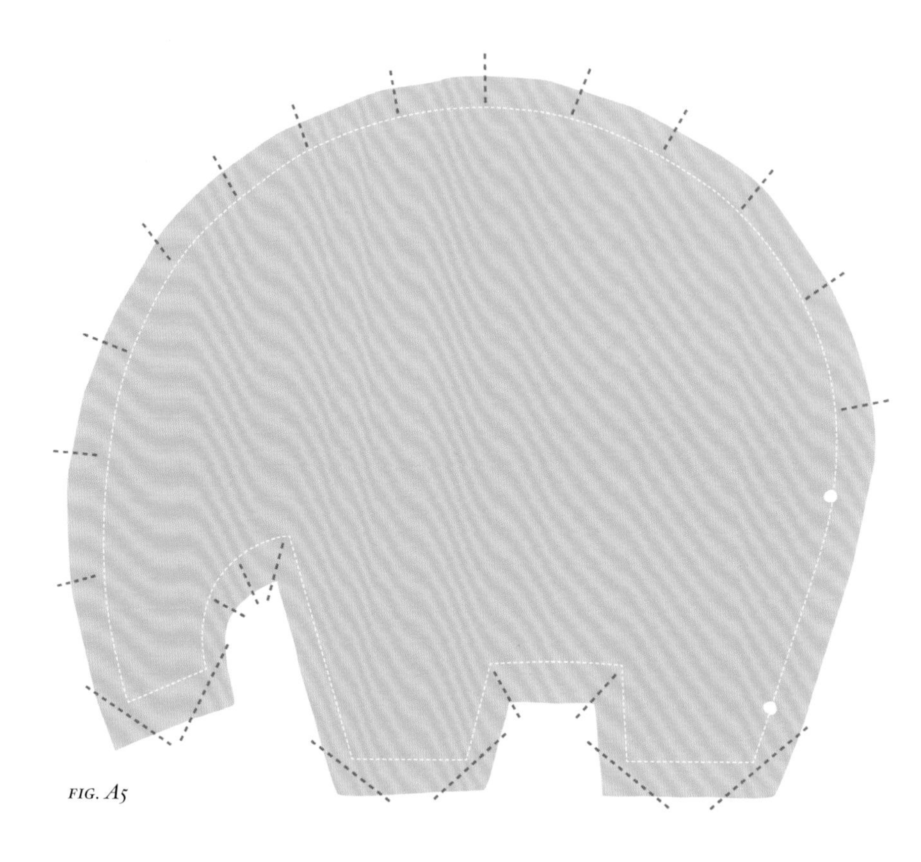

FIG. A5

THE ELEPHANT

1. Lay the elephant fabrics right sides together on a flat surface, with the elephant front on the bottom and the elephant back on the top. (Do not get this order backward, or you will have a very special elephant!) Make sure all edges are aligned.

2. Place the elephant template piece face up on top of the stacked fabric (trunk pointing to the left). Make sure that the outside edges of the template are aligned as closely as possible with the edges of your fabric.

3. Put a few pins through the two layers of fabric in the center of the elephant to hold the front and back together while you're sewing. Don't pin too close to the edges of the elephant.

4. Trace the elephant, starting at one of the black dots on the pattern, tracing around the larger part of the elephant, and finishing at the other black dot. It is important to leave an opening between the two dots, so that you can stuff the elephant after you sew.

5. Sew along the traced line.

6. Trim all the way around the elephant approximately ½" from the seam.

7. Cut the notches and trim the corners as shown (figure A5).

8. Through the opening in the elephant, flip the fabric right side out. Use a chopstick or knitting needle to push out the fabric all the way through the trunk and feet. Run the same chopstick or knitting needle around the top curve of the elephant (from the inside) to smooth out the curve. Your elephant is now ready to stuff!

9. Using a small handful of fill at a time, begin stuffing your elephant. first push the stuffing through to the tip of the trunk and into the legs. Then fill out the center. Take your time; a little extra stuffing can fill out the creases and even the lumps.

10. Time to sew up the opening. Tuck the raw edges inside and pinch the fabric shut. Make a nice crease with your fingers on both pieces of fabric. Mel's favorite way to stitch these up is by hand, with a ladder stitch (see page 176).

Finish

1. If you like, sew buttons on for the eyes of the elephant. Personally, we like to have the eyes indented in the cushion, so we sew the front and back buttons on at the same time. After anchoring one button to the fabric with a few stitches, we run the needle back and forth (through the elephant) between the two buttons, pulling them toward each other, indenting the fabric. To finish, wind the thread several times around one of the buttons and run the needle through the mound of thread underneath the button several times.

2. Trim off any excess stitches. If this gift is for a child under the age of three years, please use safety eyes or leave the buttons off entirely.

Try

Create one or both sides of your elephant out of patchwork. We did 2" patchwork squares for the pictured elephant.

GIFT CARD TRUCK SOFTIE

With four boys between us, we have a soft spot for little trucks. This delightful pillow is made from a cast-off button-down shirt. If you can find one with pockets, you can incorporate the pocket into the design and use it to hold your gift card or cash. If it doesn't have pockets, don't fret; we'll show you how to sew one onto the back. Don't have a button-down shirt available at all? Just use whatever fabric sinks your sub. Or revs your truck—har, har! Or whatever euphemism you prefer.

Have

- Cast-off button-down shirt (preferably with a pocket, but no biggie without), large enough to cut a 17" × 11" rectangle (Don't cut it yet, though!)
- Lightweight fusible interfacing if your shirt is lightweight or stretchy (We use Pellon.)
- Second piece of scrap fabric at least 17" × 11"
- Stuffing (We use Fairfield Poly-Fil.)
- Straight pins
- Truck Softie patterns (pages 180–81)

A pocketless shirt? We'll forgive you. But you'll need to have the following:

- Smaller scrap fabrics: two pieces at least 5½" × 3½" from which to cut the flap
- Another scrap piece at least 6" × 6" (from which to cut the pocket)
- Button

Optional, but Helpful

- Spray starch
- Rotary cutter or craft knife
- Cutting mat
- Straight edge, preferably a quilter's grid ruler

Prepare

1. Iron the front (and back, if you plan to use it) of the shirt. Don't bother with collars and sleeves.

2. Photocopy or print the paper pattern pieces. First prepare the truck template. Carefully cut away and discard the truck shape, but keep the page that you cut it from. (If you photocopy the pattern from the book, also cut out the surrounding rectangle as indicated.) The pattern piece should measure 17" × 11" and will have truck-shaped hole cut out. If you have to make a pocket, cut all the solid lines on your pattern and discard the flap portion, according to the instructions on the pattern.

3. Secure the placket of the shirtfront, so that the shirt pieces no longer separate when unbuttoned. We sewed one line all the way down the placket to secure it to the shirt front, but you could also use fusible web or a little fabric glue.

   TIP: If the shirt you are using is thinner, lightweight, or otherwise shifty or stretchy, feel free to use some fusible interfacing on the back. The interfacing keeps things looking neat and helps the buttons to stay where they are supposed to be. It generally avoids wonkiness.

FIG. B1

4. If the shirt has a pocket, lay the truck pattern piece over it, moving it around to find a nice placement of the pocket on the fabric. Once you've found that placement, trace the outside rectangle of the pattern piece onto the shirt. Cut out the rectangle, not the truck (figure B1).

5. If your shirt does not have a pocket, follow step 4, still finding a nice placement of the placket within the truck outline. Once you've found that placement, trace the outside rectangle of the pattern piece onto your shirt. Cut out the rectangle, not the truck.

6. Cut out one more piece of fabric for the back of your truck. It will be 17" × 11", the exact size of the piece you just cut. You can use the back side of the shirt for this, or a separate fabric.

7. If your shirt fabric doesn't include a pocket, cut out the pocket piece to the size of the pocket template. TIP: Use pinking shears, or serge or zigzag stitch the edges to keep the pocket from fraying.

Make

THE POCKET

Skip this section and go straight to The Truck if your shirt already has a pocket. The pocket flap here is optional. If you don't want a pocket flap, only follow steps 3, 4, 5, and 12. Then, move directly to the next section, The Truck.

FIG. B2

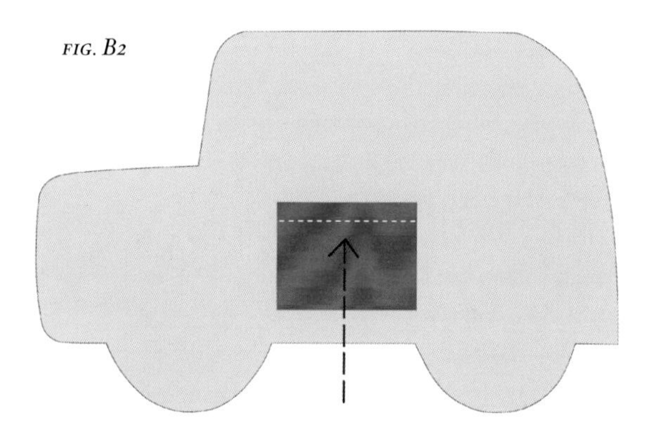

1. For the pocket flap, use two pieces of fabric that are at least 5½" × 3½". Place them right sides facing, and trace the inside shape of the pocket flap onto the center of the stacked fabric. Mark a few Xs on the top line you just traced (where you see the Xs on the pattern piece). Pin the fabric once in the center. Sew along the traced line. *Do not* sew the top line with the row of Xs. Cut

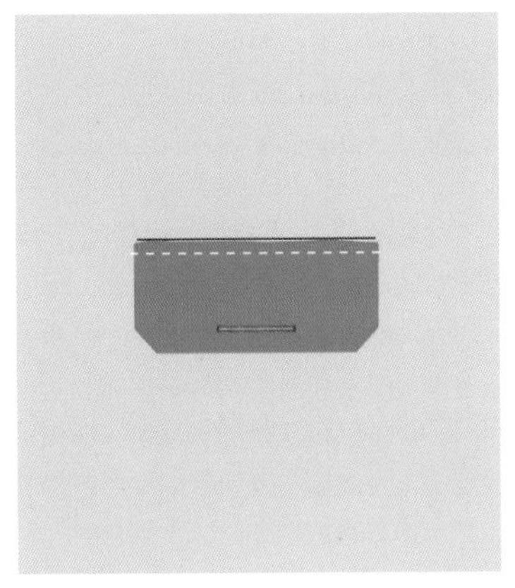

FIG. B3

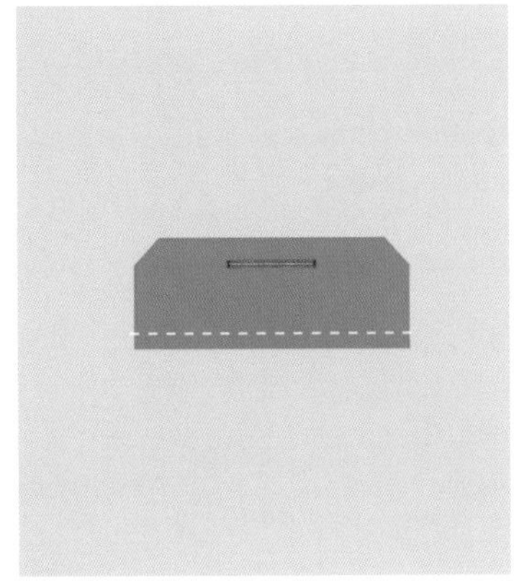

FIG. B4

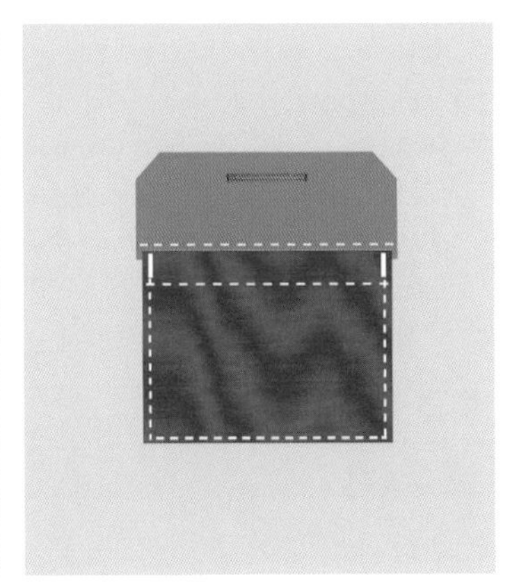

FIG. B5

directly on the top line (with the Xs) and approximately ¼" outside your sewn lines. Flip the sewn piece inside out. Use a chopstick or knitting needle to push out the corners. Iron the pocket flap flat.

2. Sew (and cut) a buttonhole in the center of the pocket flap, about ½" from the bottom. The buttonhole should be slightly wider than the button.
   TIP: Are you buttonhole challenged? Try sewing on a patch of Velcro instead. You can still stitch a pretty button to the front of the flap. It will be our little secret.

3. Find the pocket piece that you cut out. Place the pocket on your ironing board, right side down. Mist it with spray starch. Beginning with the two bottom diagonal corners, fold and iron the fabric back diagonally by ½". Then fold and iron the bottom edge and the two side edges back by ½". Finally, fold the top edge down 1", twice. Using a ¾" seam allowance, stitch once across the front top of the pocket to hold this fold down.

4. Lay the fabric for the back of the truck (the pocket side) right side up on a flat surface. Place the truck template piece face down on top (so the truck is pointed to the left), and align all the outside edges.

5. Place the pocket right side up on this fabric. It should be centered between the two truck wheels and raised about 1" toward the center of the center (figure B2).

6. Lightly draw a pencil line on the truck fabric to mark the placement of the top of the pocket, from its left edge to the right. Put the pocket and your template aside.

7. Place the pocket flap on top of the truck fabric, so that the top (unstitched) edge meets the line you just drew. The front of the flap will be face up (figure B3).

8. Sew a straight line across the top of the flap, approximately ¼" below the top edge.

9. Trim the top edge of the flap as close as you can to your new stitch (aim for approximately ⅛").

10. Flip the pocket flap all the way up (make sure all the fabric underneath remains flat, especially the large truck piece), and sew a straight line across the flap ¼" from the bottom edge (figure B4). This stitched line will hide the ragged edge.

11. Place the pocket face up on the truck fabric, so it just covers the bottom edge of the flap (figure B5).

12. Sew the pocket to the truck fabric, as close to the edge as possible (approximately ⅛" or less). Be sure to backstitch several times at the top two corners of the pocket, as the stitches will come undone over time if they are not reinforced. (Don't sew across the pocket top!)

13. Fold the flap back down, and use a pencil to mark a dot through the center of the buttonhole onto the pocket itself. This will show you where the button should go.

14. Use a needle and thread to sew the button to the pocket.

THE TRUCK

1. Lay the truck fabrics aligned right sides together on a flat surface, with the truck front on the bottom and the truck back on the top. (Do not get this backward, or your final result will be a very odd vehicle!) Make sure all edges are aligned.

2. Place the truck template piece face up on top of your stacked fabric (with the truck pointing to the right). Make sure that the outside edges of the template are aligned as closely as possible with the edges of your fabric.

3. Put a few pins through the two layers of fabric in the center of the truck to hold the front and back together while you're sewing. Don't pin too close to the edges of the truck.

4. Trace the truck, starting at one of the black dots, tracing around the larger portion of the truck, and finishing at the other black dot. It is important to leave an opening between the two dots so you can stuff the truck after you sew it.

5. Sew along the traced line.

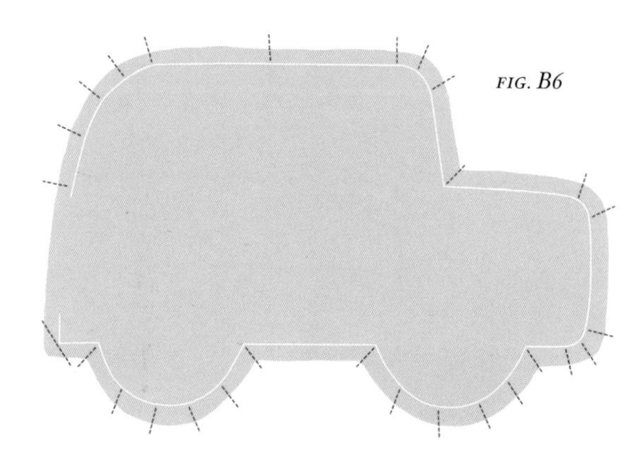

FIG. B6

6. Trim all the way around the truck, approximately ½" from the seam.

7. Cut the notches and trim the corners as shown (figure B6). Don't cut into your seam, though!

8. Through the opening in the truck, turn the fabric right side out. Use a chopstick or knitting needle to push out the fabric all the way through the wheels and the front end. Run the same chopstick or knitting needle around the perimeter of the truck (from the inside) to smooth out all the curves. Now stuff your truck!

Finish

1. Using a small handful of fill at a time, begin stuffing your truck. First push the stuffing through to the front end and into the wheels. Then fill out the top and center. Take your time; a little extra stuffing can fill out the creases and even the lumps.

2. Time to sew up the opening. Tuck the raw edges inside, and pinch the fabric shut. Make a nice crease with your fingers on both pieces of fabric. Mel's favorite way to stitch these up is by hand, with a ladder stitch (see page 176).

Try

Use an old T-shirt to make your cushions. (Just line with fusible interfacing first, to keep the fabric from stretching while you sew.)

BRASIL

THE MANNER OF GIVING IS WORTH MORE THAN THE GIFT.

PIERRE CORNEILLE, *LE MENTEUR*

EverReady

GIFT CARD WALLET

One afternoon—the one in which Mel's dog Buddy Holly tried to swallow a sewing needle and we had to pull it out of his tongue, and boy, wasn't *that* fun?—we sat down to work on more projects. Melody had the basics to put this gift-wrapping idea together and insisted there was something in them. I, ready to wind down, was just insisting on a glass of wine. She won. And from super simple pieces, this little wallet was born. The finished product looks like you spent much time and effort in making it, and the recipient will never guess it costs nearly nothing and takes very little time. But not only is the wallet easy to make, it is also cute as pie. Or manly, if you make it that way.

You'll likely have way more thoughts on the various uses or reuses for this wallet than we could ever fit in a book. It's a great business card holder! Instant hip wallet! Keep a love note in it! Kids love these, too, for their coveted allowance. Those cards from yogurt, sandwich, or ice cream shops that get punched for each purchase, and then you get a free something, or half off? My son likes to collect those and keep them in one of our prototypes for this project. It's just right.

Have

- Any scrap fabric or paper larger than 6" × 8"—old book pages from lonely, forgotten books; magazine pages; children's art (maybe the fridge is beginning to suffocate?), comic books, origami paper, and so on all work well.
- Clear contact paper
- Velcro
- Ruler or straight edge
- Craft knife or sharp scissors

Optional, and Awesome

- Japanese tape
- Stickers
- Stamps and ink of any colors
- Markers
- Any other fun paper ephemera

Prepare

Gather the materials you are going to use. Use whole sheets of paper or assemble several sheets into a collage. Accessorize! Add tape, apply stickers, draw, paint; you get the idea.

TIP: If you layer papers, make sure you stick down the entire surface of the paper (not just the edges) with glue or other adhesive. Your final sheet needs to be at least 5½" × 7½". Also, one of our better tricks is to make a sheet way larger than this so that the final is cut diagonally from somewhere in the middle.

Make

1. Cut out two pieces of clear contact paper, just a little larger than your sheet of paper.

2. Peel the backing off one sheet of contact paper, place it adhesive side up on a clean work surface, and place your decorated paper neatly in the center. Peel the other contact sheet, and place it adhesive side down on your decorated paper. Use your hands to smooth out any bubbles, starting in the center and working your way out to the edges.

3. Trim your paper down to 5¼" × 7¼". (This is where, if your original sheet is large, you can cut at odd angles to make your design even more interesting.)

4. From the bottom, fold the paper up 2¾", and make a sharp crease. Be sure you like it because this will be the front of the wallet.

5. Sew this piece down on the left and right sides to create the pocket. Use a straight or decorative stitch with a ¼" seam allowance.

6. Now fold 1¼" down from the top to create the front flap, make a sharp crease, and open it back up.

Finish

1. With the top flap open, affix a ½" square of adhesive Velcro to the top left and right corners.

2. Stick the Velcro mates directly on top of these two pieces. Peel off the adhesive backs, and firmly press the flap closed, allowing the mates to stick in their proper place on the wallet.

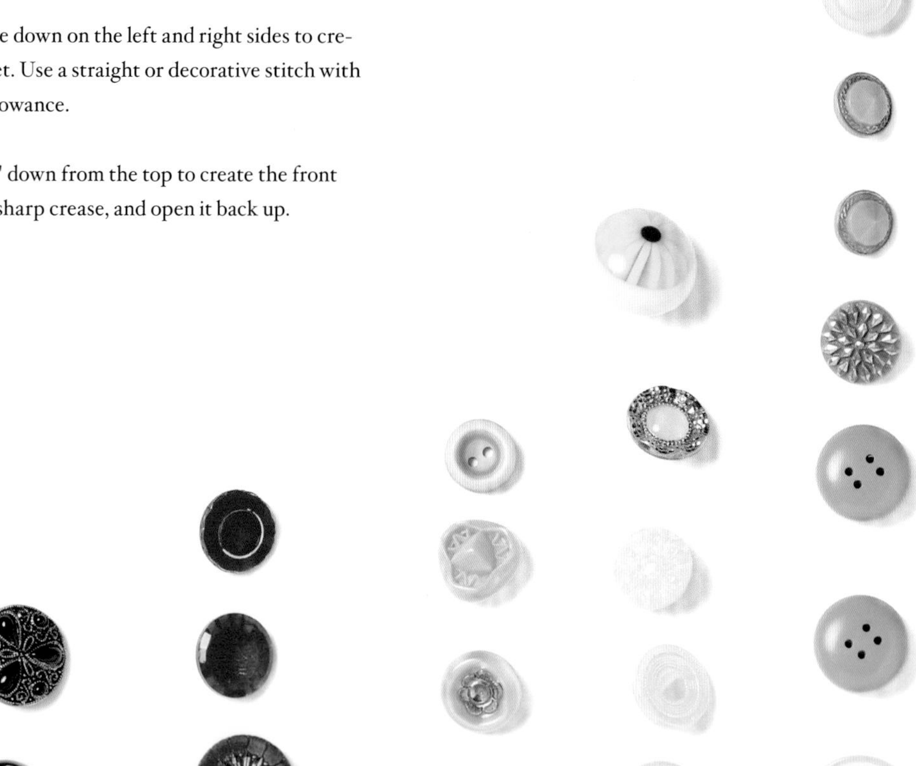

Try

- Instead of stitching down the edges, use pretty Japanese tape (or any other kind of tape) to secure the pocket.
- We used Therm-O-Web iron-on vinyl to laminate a vintage fabric scrap, trimmed it down to size, and sewed it up following the directions above. Just for kicks, and because we needed a little excitement, we added a buttonhole and button to this version.

But Wait! There's More!

Instead of making softies in the shapes of elephants and trucks, make a simple square or rectangular pillow, with a really cool silhouette appliquéd to the front and a pocket on the back. This super-stylish pillow can be given as a housewarming gift (holding a card from a home improvement store, naturally), or it can be made to match a baby's nursery colors (holding a gift card from the store where the mommy-to-be is registered). A high school graduate might love a larger roll pillow, to sit against while studying away at school. You can include a gift card for a coffee shop, iTunes, or a grocery store. Man, I would have loved a prepaid phone card *before* my Dad got the first $500 phone bill (I still have nightmares), way back when. Before cell phones with calling plans. Or even cell phones.

IF THE GIFT IS SMALL, SOFT, OR SQUISHY

Some of the best presents are squishy and small, soft, and just feel good to touch and hold. We are suckers for teeny newborn-sized onesies. I almost have to give one to any friend having a baby. This past Christmas I found and ordered a soft, hand-knit Oscar the Grouch hat with a matching scarf and mittens for our four-year-old.

When the gift is too hard to wrap in paper, these boxes and bags are the perfect solution. From juggling balls to adorable felt plushies, fat quarters of fabric, and socks with each toe a different color, these clever hideaways are your go-to wrapping solutions. You could even use these projects to wrap that monogrammed toilet paper meant "For the Hostess Who Has Everything" (just be sure to know your recipient's sense of humor *really* well. I sent some of this to my mother once for her birthday, but she thought I was insinuating what one could do to her name, and therefore, her personal self. Be wary.).

Your start to these packages is likely in your pantry. There are boxes in there of all sorts, shapes, and sizes. At my house, they are usually already empty. Just a fun little thing the kids like to do. Finish off the last of the sesame rice crackers, and just let the box *sit* there. With nothing in it. To torture me. Digressing. . . . For the drawstring bag, skip the pantry and head back to your sewing/crafting stash for some fabric scraps.

For second and third lives, the pantry box projects can hold tools on desks, at vanities, or on craft tables. For a birthday party grill out, I used a shorter pantry box to hold plastic utensils or rolled up napkins. Melody has uncountable bits of trims, ribbons, and other notions to dress up these boxes, and they are also super-cute receptacles for keeping plastic grocery sacks, for later use, or to stash dog treats. Sometimes, the pantry gets those little moths, and you have to enclose your grains in plastic bags. Drop your favorite zipped-up cereal back into a recycled, fabric-covered cereal box, and it's come full circle!

PLUCKY PANTRY BOX

We love how easily an empty box from the pantry can become such great gift wrap. Cereal, pasta, hot chocolate, breakfast bars, crackers, popcorn, cookies—the variety of boxes is endless. One of our favorites is the toaster pastries box from Trader Joe's (Melody's kids love these, so there's always a box available). This past Christmas when we had prototypes coming out our ears, Blake and I used a cereal box to give our parents homemade photo books, which no, are neither small, nor soft, nor squishy, but worked nonetheless! Note: Very few grandparents can resist entire books of their grandchildren. Easy + impactful + inexpensive = SCORE.

Have

- Empty food box from your pantry
- Fabric scraps
- Fusible web (We use Pellon Wonder Under, regular weight.)
- Iron
- Hot glue (or craft glue)

Optional, but Helpful

- Rotary cutter and cutting mat
- Ruler
- Fusible web

Prepare

1. Carefully open all the glued seams of your pantry box, so the entire box is one long flat piece. If the paper peels a bit, it's OK. If there are any raised blobs of glue left on the surface of the box, see if you can peel them off. (You just need a fairly even surface under the fabric; it doesn't have to be perfect!)

2. If the box has any small tabs for closure, like at the top of a cereal box, go ahead and trim them off.

3. Find a piece of fabric larger than the flattened box, by at least 2" on every side. This can be a solid piece or a patchwork with the seams ironed open. You can add on trims or appliqué as well.

4. Iron fusible web to the back of the fabric, and peel off the paper backing. If you need to trim rough edges off your fabric to make a nice, neat rectangle, do so now.

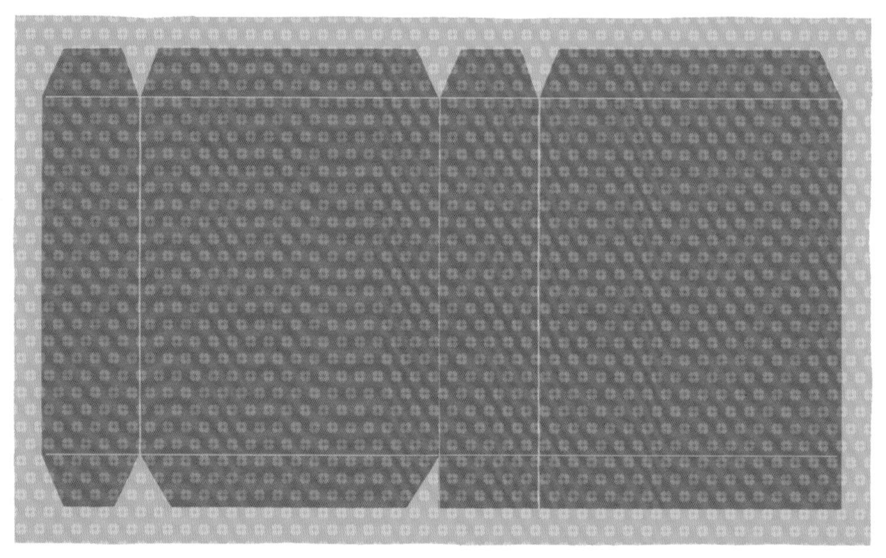

FIG. D1

Make

1. Place your fabric on top of the box, fusible side down. If the box has a slick side, it will be best to adhere the fabric to the opposite (nonslick) side. Make sure the fabric hangs over all edges of the box evenly. Iron down (figure D1).

   TIP: Place parchment paper or the peeled backing from your fusible web under the overhanging edges of the fabric so you don't iron the edges of the fabric to the ironing board.

2. Flip over the box and fabric.

3. Make vertical cuts in the fabric between each tab to separate the tabs from each other. Then make two horizontal cuts on each side to separate the side panels from the top and bottom tabs (figure D2).

4. Fold the fabric neatly over the two side edges and each tab, and iron it down.

5. Use scissors or a craft knife to shape the short, diagonal, side edges of the top and bottom flaps (figure D3).

6. If you have any ragged edges, trim them. If you are concerned about fraying on the edges you just cut, use a small bead of craft or paper glue on your finger, and smooth it along the edges.

7. Reassemble the side and bottom of the box, and stick it together tight with hot glue.

Finish

1. Cut a piece of ribbon long enough to wrap under and around the box, and tie on top.

2. Secure it to the sides and bottom of the box using thinly cut strips of fusible web (Stitch Witchery works great here) or craft or hot glue. If you use fusible web, place the thin strip between the ribbon and the box. Touch the outside of the ribbon lightly with your iron on the silk setting to adhere. The ribbon will tie up into a sweet bow at the top of the box, and hold the top flaps closed.

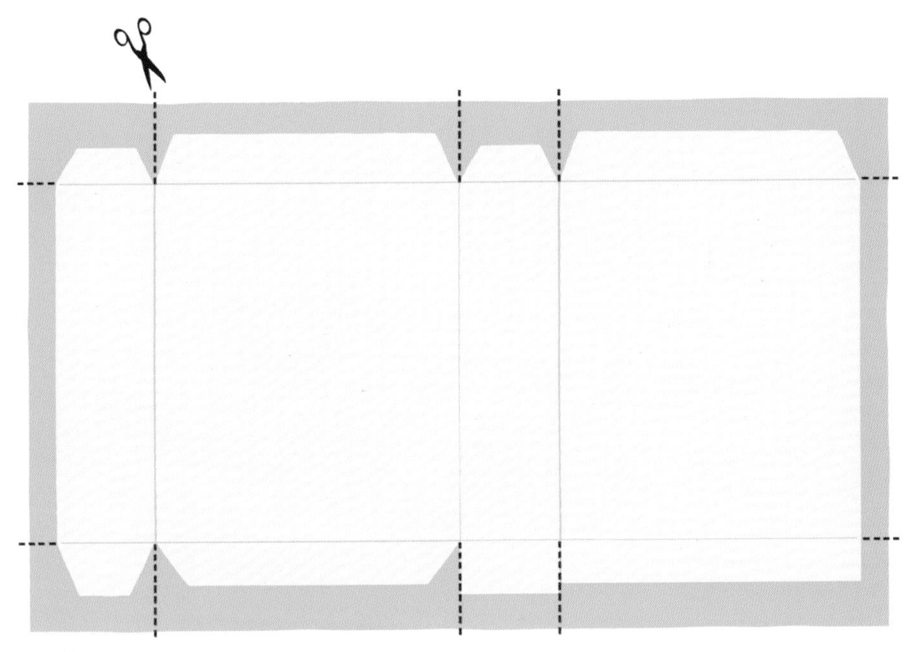

FIG. D2

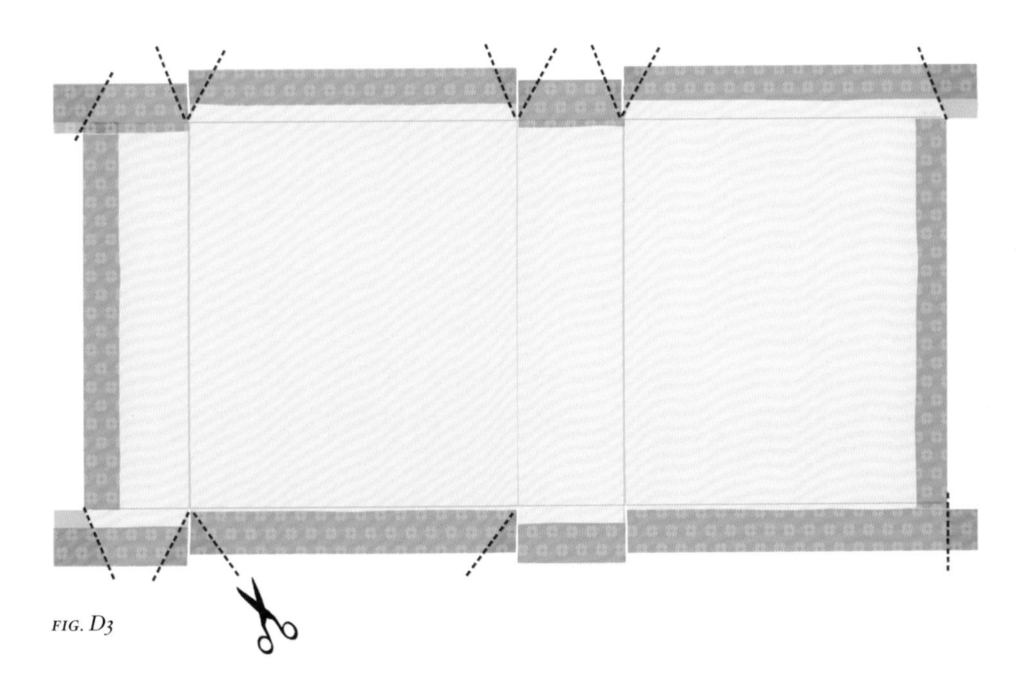

FIG. D3

Try

- This same project works beautifully using decorative paper and spray adhesive or decoupage glue. Follow all steps above, substituting paper for fabric. To adhere the paper to the box, use spray adhesive (or you can evenly coat the back of the paper with craft glue). After you apply the adhesive, keep a piece of parchment paper under your project to keep the paper from sticking to your work surface.

  TIP: If using spray adhesive, coat the back of your paper entirely and spray a fine mist over the box itself. The glue sticks to itself beautifully for an extra-firm hold.
- If you're using a tall, thin box (like a cereal box), you may find it helpful to reassemble and cut the box so it lays flat, with the largest surfaces acting as the top and bottom of the box (think: cigar box). If you do this, the top will lift open to reveal the entire inside of the box, which you may want to line with paper or fabric.
- Try reusing and decorating an oatmeal container or coffee tin here, too.

RANCH
WAGON
ORIGINAL

A PLACE FOR EVERYTHING,
EVERYTHING IN ITS PLACE.

✿ BENJAMIN FRANKLIN ✿

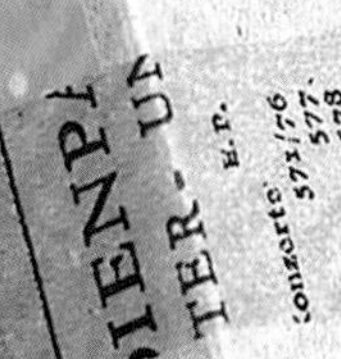

INSIDE-OUT BOX

This project, while much like the Plucky Pantry Box, is deceptively simple. All you're doing here is opening up a pantry box and reassembling it inside out. A few added embellishments or accessories, however, make it one of the loveliest packages you will ever give.

Have

- Empty food box from your pantry
- Hot glue
- Craft glue
- Assortment of pretty paper, decorative tape, stickers, fabric scraps and fusible web for appliqué, embroidery thread and needle, ribbon, and any of the accessories from The Extras chapter

Prepare

Carefully open all the glued seams of your pantry box so the entire box is one long flat piece. While some ripping is inevitable, just try to minimize it as much as you can. If there are any raised blobs of glue left on the surface of the box, see if you can peel them off.

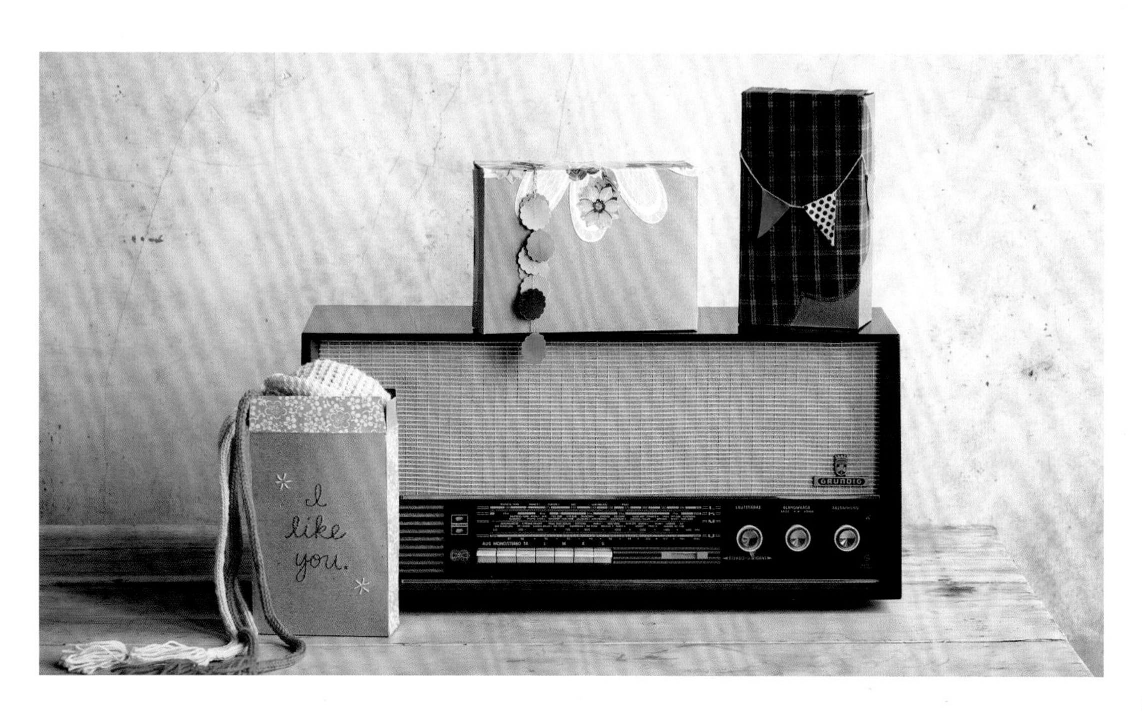

Make

1. The brown interior of your box is now going to be the exterior. We love letting the brown surface speak for itself. However, the goal is to cover up any ugly spots with pretty paper or stickers or decorative tape. Get creative! Here are some suggestions.

   - Iron fusible web to the wrong side of your scrap fabric, and cut out an interesting shape. Iron this shape to your box. Use a sewing machine to applique stitch around the edges of the fabric. You can even "draw" on your box using stitches from your machine. (Melody loves sewing on paper, or lightweight cardboard!)
   - Add decorative tape to make pretty stripes around the box. Try making them diagonal!
   - Cut out a lovely image, and evenly coat the back with craft glue or spray adhesive. Cover any ripped areas of the box with this creative concealer.
   - Sometimes the top tab and flaps get a little beat up. I like to stick down something new over the entire flap (decorative tape or paper both work well here), and then, from the backside, carefully cut off any excess bits that are overhanging the original flap. This extra layer makes the opening of the box stronger.
   - We've even embroidered directly onto the box. To do this, lightly pencil in a line drawing or simple message. Using an embroidery needle, poke holes along your lines, about ⅛" apart. Thread the needle with embroidery floss, and backstitch through the holes.

2. Reassemble the side and bottom of the box, and stick the flaps tight with hot glue. The top tab should hold the box shut, just like it did in your pantry.

Finish

Add accessories from The Extras chapter. We used Festive Flag Garland, Paper Punch Garland, and Newspaper Flower in some of our projects.

SIMPLE DRAWSTRING BAG

Now we're going to take a minute to extol the virtues of the humble drawstring bag. Very few things would *not* work in a drawstring bag. A cake. A cake would not work in a drawstring bag. Unless it was in a cake box, and *carefully* toted in a drawstring bag. Unprotected crystal would not work in a drawstring bag. But crystal *in a box* would work in a drawstring bag. A flock of birds would not work in a drawstring bag. But a pair of canaries in a lovely cage, *draped with a drawstring bag*, and tied at the bottom? Sublime.

In working out these projects, Melody and I have found ourselves with quite a few drawstring bags of all shapes and sizes. From the 5-Minute Party Pouches (see page 127) to much larger bags, these handy items comprise a large portion of our gift-wrapping stash. They are so simple to make and can be used to wrap nearly anything.

After our families exchange presents for holidays, we all swap the bags around again and store them for future gift giving. We have so many bags now that we keep finding new uses for them: to help organize suitcases when we travel, I keep Velcro rollers in one, a new pair of sandals in another (so my in-laws' dog won't chew them to bits when they visit). I made one specifically for my son's asthma medications, and it hangs on the side of the fridge to remind us to use it daily, as well as for easy retrieval of his emergency meds. When he stays at his grandparents', I don't have to hunt all over the house gathering the this and the that. I just grab the bag! Melody's daughter Iliana uses one to gather together her most special little stuffed animals, and my husband keeps a tangle of cords for who-knows-what in another. The drawstring bag rocks. If you're in a hurry and need one go-to gift-wrapping project, the drawstring bag will work nearly every time.

One of our favorite drawstring bags has a simple shirred top (which, I suppose, would no longer make it a drawstring bag). If you'd like to make a classic drawstring bag (with an actual drawstring), see the variation at the end.

Have

- Fabric
- Elastic thread
- Iron
- Straight pins

Optional, but Helpful
- Rotary cutter and cutting mat
- Spray bottle of water

Prepare

Decide how big you want your bag to be. Add 1" to the width and 3½" to the height, and cut two pieces of fabric to this dimension. To make a bag 7" × 10", we cut our fabric to 8" × 13½". To prevent fraying, cut the fabric with pinking shears, or zigzag stitch or serge the edges.

Make

1. Placing your fabric right sides together, sew around the side and bottom edges with a ½" seam allowance.

2. If possible, iron your seams to one side (sometimes this can be difficult with very small bags).
   OPTIONAL: From the outside of the bag, top stitch along each seam. First, make sure the edges of the fabric underneath your seam are pressed to the side that you plan to stitch on. Stitch about ⅛" along the seam from the outside of your bag, being sure to stitch through the seam allowance underneath. This stitching will reinforce your seams and make your bag sturdier (figure F1).

3. Fold the top edge under, toward the wrong side, by 3". Iron a sharp crease.

4. Wind some elastic thread into your bobbin. You'll do this by hand. Don't stretch it too tight as you're winding. Put the bobbin in your machine.

5. Put regular thread on your spool. Set your machine to the longest stitch, and set your tension to the highest number.

6. With a 1½" seam allowance, begin stitching around the top of the bag. You will be stitching through the top layer as well as the folded-under layer. Be sure to reverse your stitch at the beginning to keep the elastic from unraveling. As you make your way around to the place where you began stitching, gradually increase your seam allowance so that you're doing a spiral around the bag, with each new line being approximately ¼" below the one before it (figure F2). As you're sewing over sections that are already gathered, try to pull the fabric straight as much as possible. After you've sewn three to five rows of shirring, end your stitch on the same side where you began about 2 to 2½" from the top edge. We're sewing down the bag, not up, so the measurement will be larger. Be sure to reverse stitch at the very end (figure F2).

Finish

1. If the fabric isn't as gathered as you would like, mist it with a little water and watch it gather like magic!

2. While you still have your elastic thread in your machine, why not make some Resplendent Roses (see The Extras chapter) to embellish your bag?

3. Don't forget to remove the elastic thread and return your machine to its normal settings!

FIG. F1

FIG. F2

VARIATION

And then, there is this version. This classic drawstring bag is just as lovely, and you can tie it up with a bow.

Have

- Fabric
- Ribbon
- Iron

Optional, but Helpful

- Rotary cutter and cutting mat

Make

1. Follow the Make steps 1–3 on page 38, but unfold the top edge after making the crease with your iron.

2. On the front of the bag, sew (and cut) two vertical buttonholes, side by side, about 1½" below that crease. Refold the top of the bag.

3. Sew two seams all the way around the bag (through both layers of fabric), one above the buttonholes and one below. These seams will create the channel for your ribbon to run through.

4. Attach a safety pin to the end of your ribbon, and run it through the channel—in one buttonhole and out the other. Add your gift, and tie it up pretty!

Try

For one more variation on the drawstring bag (and because we love options), follow the original Make steps 1–3. With the top edge still folded down, pin a wide ribbon 2" from the top edge horizontally through both layers around the top of the bag, leaving a ½" gap between the two ends at the front of the bag. This will be the channel for the drawstring. Stitch along the top and bottom edges of this ribbon (stitching through the folded layer of the top of the bag as well). Now run a skinnier ribbon through the wide ribbon and tie in the front. The two ribbons add an extra decorative touch to your bag!

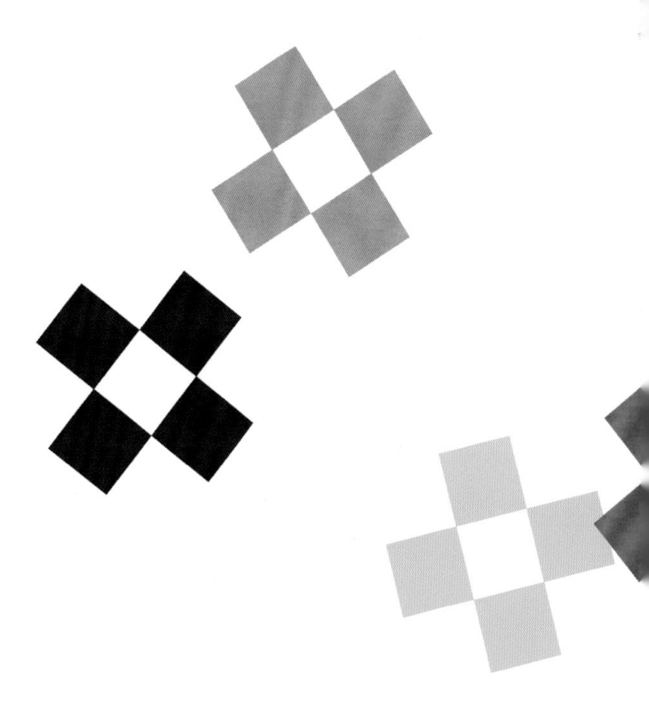

But Wait! There's More!

These projects, like the entire book, are just meant to be inspiration. Other shapes, materials, and potential present-packaging gems are lurking in your kitchen. Oatmeal canisters, tin cans, among others. You could have a pillow-case that looks pretty good already that could quickly be transformed into a roomy drawstring bag. If a project calls for ribbon, you can sub with twine, or make your own ribbon from The Extras chapter. If your gift is a bit large for one of the boxes in your pantry, try deconstructing two of the same shape and size, and putting them back together as a larger package. If what you have in your house is not handmade ribbon but lengths of curling ribbon, use it. The point is to creatively, beautifully put something together from what is in *your* space, including the wrapping paper you might already have, which would work splendidly on the outside of the Plucky Pantry Box. If you have it, use it! ♛

VANDENBERG AFB. CA
OCT 6
1978
15¢
OLIVER WENDELL HOLMES
NAVSTAR-I
VANDENBERG AFB. CA
FEB 22
1978
LIBERTY NATIONAL LIFE INSURANCE COMPANY
A Company with a Creed!
"Since its organization in 1900, the guiding principle of Liberty National Life Insurance Company has been to achieve success by deserving it; to protect its policyholders and their beneficiaries with a fair, unselfish contract and to construe it liberally in their favor; to serve them faithfully, adequately, honestly and economically."
Our policies may be secured for only a few cents per week for your entire family.
A representative of this Company is a resident of your community.
Call him for complete information.
DIX AND RANDS
HIGH GRADE
SHARPS
3/9
BEST QUALITY
DISTRICT OFFICE ADDRE
14755
CUSTOMER'S SLIP
Date Left
Date Promised
Paid
Due
Number Rolls
Negatives
Size
Jumbo Prints Cost Only a Few Pennies More
No. 14755
NOTE: All complaints must be returned with this envelope and original contents. We are only responsible for the retail price of film in case of loss.
Name
Address
Date Left
Date Promised
Number Rolls
Negatives
Size
each Contact
each Jumbo
each 4x6 Jumbo
each size Enlargement
each
Special
Paid
Due
Total $
DEALER:
LET SNAPSHOTS PRESERVE THE STORY
FIRST DAY

THERE ARE ALSO GIFTS THAT ARE SUPER THIN OR FLAT

My husband is a gigantic fan of the animated series *King of the Hill*. Being that he is from Texas, Hank Hill is his hero. Last year for his birthday, I found a print of Hank signed by the series' creator, Mike Judge. It came in the mail, in a manila envelope, and that is precisely how I gave it to him. That was *before* we came up with all these fab wrap ideas!

These projects go perfectly with photos, art prints, and even homemade gift certificates. This project collection will require some lovely or quirky books from which you are willing to cut the guts. You want the covers, not the pages, unless you see pages that would make great pockets. Save those. Put the rest of the pages away for another day. Your collection of decorative tapes will come in handy, as will scrap fabrics, again. And a vintage game with most of its pieces missing will also become a part of a package as wonderful as whatever is tucked inside.

It's also easy to reuse these projects around the house. When I visited friends in New York, they had a little stack of Metro cards on an entry table, an easy place to find them when they were needed. One of these Recycled Readers would have worked really well sitting right there, holding the cards. The Game Board Box is a great way to collect clutter. We always need a dumping place for keys, wallets, glasses, and those super critical, cannot-throw-them-away wadded up pieces of paper and lint from pockets at the end of a work day. And who doesn't need some sort of receptacle for all the stuff that comes through the laundry? I have two Lego heads, one paper clip, a handful of loose change, some really clean but now tattered chewing gum wrapping, and several marbles rolling around on top of my dryer right now.

These projects are also great for saving keepsakes. If I could find the ticket stubs I've saved *somewhere* over the years from movies Blake and I have seen together, they'd be great in a Recycled Reader or small Game Board Box. I have one box that I keep hidden in the closet just for little written things Blake has given me over the years and another for the photos of friends' kids (the ones we *really* like).

40267
801557
ZEPHRAM BIDS FAREWELL TO HIS SWEETHEART AT THE SPACEPORT
WAGON-TRAIN TO THE STARS
A 3-D PRODUCTION
"A NEW HOME ON MARS"
FOLLOW OUR YOUNG EXPLORER AS HE LEAVES THE COMFORTS OF HIS EARTHLY HOME TO PIONEER A BOLD NEW FUTURE ON OUR NEIGHBORING RED PLANET — MARS!
LEARNING TO SOLDER
A 3-D PRODUCTION
"YOUNG ENGINEERS EXPLORATORIUM"
A STRAIGHT SPINE IS ESSENTIAL
A 3-D PRODUCTION
"PUTTING YOUR BEST FOOT FORWARD"
06
Macaroon
HAPPY HAPPY
BIRTHDAY!

RECYCLED READER

We haunt thrift stores. If you've not discovered them, they are full of wonderful books that you might never read—or that may be impossible to read because the pages are just so tattered. Some of these have gorgeous covers. Vintage children's books are perfect here when the pages have been chewed and scribbled. We have found the *Reader's Digest* Condensed Books series from the '50s and '60s to have some of the most beautiful covers ever. We smile every time we pull out one to work with. But then, we're odd. Often, veteran books are a few dollars a dozen, as collectors have no interest in them for their literary value. This project creates an adorable folder of sorts that holds great little (and thin) gifts and is reusable as a wonderful mini-scrapbook.

You can choose whatever size book you want for the gift you are giving. And depending on that size, the number and dimensions of the pockets are up to you. Stick stickers, glue down trims, and add all the Japanese tape that makes you happy. The final product will hold photos, vintage ephemera, a collection of concert ticket stubs, an array of stickers, or pretty craft papers. I recently was given a few keepsakes from my late grandfather's old rolltop, like his mother's Delta Airlines ticket from the early '50s (cross country, *nineteen dollars round trip, y'all!*). When this book project winds down, I'm making a Recycled Reader for those treasures.

Have

- Great old book that no one is reading (And hey, save a few pages for the Gift Card Wallet!)
- Scrap papers (Heavier stock works best.)
- Craft glue or spray adhesive
- Straight edge
- Wide tape (at least 1", preferably wider)
- Craft knife

Optional

- Ribbon
- Decorative tape
- Stamps, stickers, decorative paper, ephemera
- Fabric trims
- And on, and on

Prepare

OUTSIDE COVER

1. Use a straight edge and a craft knife to neatly cut the front and back covers off of the book.

2. Place each cover face up and side by side, leaving a ¼" gap between them. The back cover should be on left, and the front cover on right, so the book closes correctly in the end.

3. Use a wide piece of decorative tape (no less than 1") to cover the gap, leaving an extra 3" hanging off the top and bottom.

TIP: It helps to run tape down one of covers first, and then carefully smooth it over to the other cover. It can be hard to do both at same time without one cover slipping. Be sure to carefully align the top and bottom edges of the covers while affixing the tape.

4. Flip over the taped-together covers, and wrap the overhanging tape pieces around the edges and onto the inside of these covers. Add another piece of tape in between the inside covers to reinforce the tape and cover any exposed sticky parts.

5. Open and close the covers several times to be sure they line up nicely. We will refer to this piece as your Outside Cover.

ENDPAPER

1. With the two covers lying open, measure the width and height of both covers together.

2. Subtract ¼" from each of those measurements, and make note of this final figure. For example, if the overall measurement was 11" × 8", then jot down 10¾" × 7¾".

3. Cut a piece of paper (heavier paper or card stock works best) to this measurement.

4. Lay this paper face down horizontally. Using a ruler, find the center of the paper, and lightly draw a vertical line down the center where the paper will fold once it is affixed to the book covers. Using a craft knife and a straight edge, lightly score this line. This light cut will help the page to fold in half neatly.

5. Cover this scored line with a piece of masking tape or clear tape to keep the paper from tearing with extended use.

6. Go ahead and fold the paper to form a sharp crease. We will refer to this piece as your Endpaper.

POCKET(S)

1. Decide how many pockets you want and how big they will be. For each measurement, add 1½" to the width and ¾" to the height.

2. Using the measurement you just came up with, cut a piece of cardstock or heavy paper to this size. If you think the top edge of your pocket needs extra reinforcing (will the paper tear with extended use?), run a piece of decorative (or clear) tape across the top edge horizontally and fold it over to the back.

3. Fold the two sides and bottom edges under by ¾". TIP: If the paper is heavy, you can lightly score the fold lines on the front of the paper. This will help it to fold neatly. Also, it may be helpful to clip the bottom two corners off (where the fold lines overlap) before folding.

4. Apply either double-sided tape or a thin line of glue to the ¾" flaps. (Be sure you apply this glue to the outside of the folded flaps. You want to glue the flaps to the endpaper, not to the back of the pocket!) Then secure the pocket to the endpaper you just made, placing it where you like.

5. Make and add other pockets as necessary.

Make

1. The endpaper you made now needs to be affixed to the outside cover. We coated the back of the endpaper with spray adhesive, but you could also use craft glue.

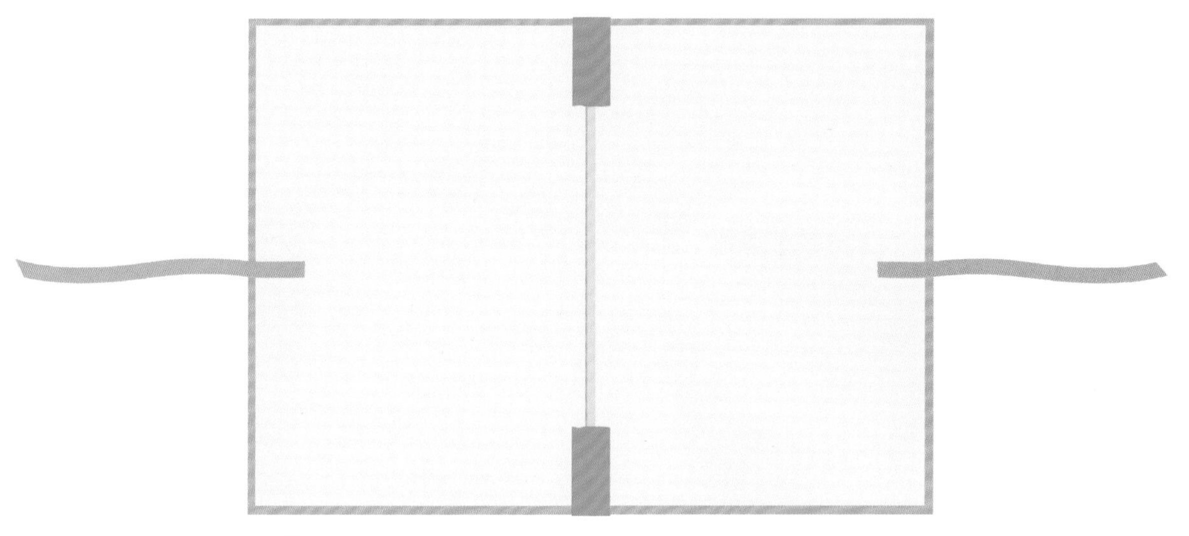

FIG. G1

TIP: If you are using spray adhesive, do one very light mist on the outside cover itself (where the endpaper will be affixed), and another light mist on the endpaper. Spray adhesive sticks to itself extremely well. If you are using liquid glue, use a small piece of scrap cardboard or an index card to evenly spread glue all over the endpaper, coating it from edge to edge.

2. Open the outside cover on your work surface, with the unfinished inside facing up (make sure it is not upside down).
   OPTIONAL: If you like, secure a piece of ribbon to the left and right edge of the unfinished inside of the outside cover before you glue on the endpapers. When the covers close, you can tie the ribbon to hold the book shut (figure G1).

3. The endpaper is just a bit smaller than the outside cover and should stick down about ⅛" from all the outer edges. Begin by carefully floating the top edge of the endpapers just below the top edge of the outside cover. Make sure everything looks evenly aligned.

4. Very carefully lower the endpaper, being sure that it stays straight. Does it look good? Smooth it down securely.

FINISH

Add the gifts and go!

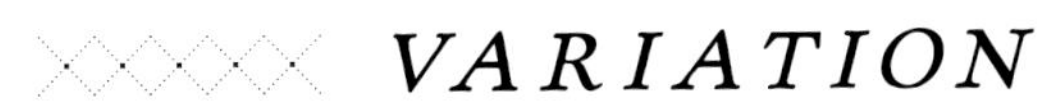

VARIATION

This is just a variation of the previous project, but using fabric instead of papers. All previous knowledge applies. Go to it.

Have

- Great old hardcover book (Don't take one from someone's nightstand!)
- Chipboard, cardstock, or thin cardboard at least as large as the two book covers when laying side by side (Stuck for ideas? Try a cereal box!)
- Scrap fabrics: one piece larger than the chipboard above, and several smaller pieces for pockets
- Fusible web, preferably heavy duty, but regular is OK too (No fusable web? Try decoupage glue!)
- Craft glue or spray adhesive
- Straight edge
- Decorative tape
- Craft knife
- Scissors, regular or pinking shears
- Straight pins
- Decorative trims, lace, or ribbon, if you like

Prepare

OUTSIDE COVER

Follow all of the Outside Cover instructions from the Recycled Reader.

ENDPAPER

1. Follow steps 1–6 from the Endpaper instructions from the Recycled Reader, being sure to use thin cardboard, chipboard, or heavy cardstock.

2. Next, choose fabric for the endpaper, and cut out a piece that is larger than the cardboard by at least 1" on each side (the top, left, right, and bottom).

3. Fold the fabric in half, left to right, and lightly iron a crease, just so you can see the center. This fabric will be your endpaper.

THE POCKET(S)

1. Decide the size of pockets, add 1" to the width and 2½" to the height of each (for example, if you want a finished pocket to be 3" × 5", cut out a piece of fabric 4" × 7½").
   TIP: To keep the inside pocket edges from fraying, cut the fabric with pinking shears, or zigzag stitch or serge the edges.

2. Mist the back of fabric with spray starch; fold the left, right, and bottom edges over by ½"; and iron them down.

3. Fold the top edge down 1", twice, so that the edge of the fabric isn't visible. Sew this edge down with a ¾" seam allowance.

4. Pin the pocket(s) onto the chosen fabric for the endpaper. In placing the pocket, remember that your final endpaper, once in place, will be at least 1" smaller on each of the outside edges. You can use the center crease in the fabric for reference.

5. Once the pocket(s) are placed and pinned, stitch them to the endpaper on the left, right, and bottom edges, as close to the edges as possible.
   TIP: Remember! When sewing a pocket, always reinforce the stitch several times at the top two corners so the fabric doesn't pull away over time. Make as many pockets as you like. Pockets are cute. We like pockets.

6. Place the endpaper fabric (with its pockets sewn on) right side down on the ironing board, iron heavy-duty fusible web to the wrong side of the fabric, and remove the paper backing.

7. Line up the center crease of the endpapers with the center crease of chipboard, and carefully iron the fabric to the chipboard.
   TIP: The 1" overhanging fabric will have fusible web on the back. Do not iron this down to your ironing board. You can put the original piece of backing from the fusible web under the part you are ironing to keep it from sticking.

8. Flip over the chipboard and fabric, and trim off the corners of the overhanging fabric.

9. Fold the edges of the fabric around the chipboard, and then iron them neatly in place.
   TIP: If you don't have fusible web, you can coat the chipboard with decoupage glue and carefully adhere the fabric.

Make

Follow the Make steps 1–4 from the Recycled Reader.

Finish

Add gifts. Go.

Try

If you don't have a great book cover but you do have some wonderful fabric, make your own book cover by wrapping sturdy cardboard or chipboard with fabric. You can use two separate pieces of chipboard, or one large piece scored down the middle and folded into the two covers. Back your fabric with fusible web, and iron it to the surface of your chipboard, making sure you have at least a 1" overhang on each edge to wrap around the back. And again, try decoupage glue. Where does it not work?!

EACH DAY COMES BEARING ITS OWN GIFTS.
UNTIE THE RIBBONS.
RUTH ANN SCHABACKER

PRETTY PRINT KEEPER

One of our favorite gifts? Signed prints by independent artists. Melody has them in almost every room of her house. I don't. Yet. I've only recently become aware of the vast, amazing resource in beautiful prints on websites like etsy and from other sources like homegrown craft fairs, local art shows, and even flea markets and thrift stores. When you buy a print, you're not only helping an artist to make a living, but you're getting a lovely piece of art at a very reasonable price.

And when you're ready to give one of these prints as a gift? Leave it in the tube, but don't forget to make it pretty. Use decorative paper, wallpaper, or fabric to spiff it up. Save tube mailers you might receive, or pick up a few the next time you are at a post office or shipping store. They are sturdy, simple to decorate, and are an excellent way to store artwork.

Next time you're looking for the perfect gift, consider a lovely, whimsical print by a local artist.

Have

- Paper
- Spray adhesive, decoupage glue, or double-sided tape
- Mailing tube

Prepare

1. Measure the tube from top to bottom. If it has any ridges at the top or bottom edges (this includes the lid), measure between the ridges (that is, between the lip of the lid and the metal or plastic ring that usually protects the bottom of the tube). That measurement will be the height of your paper.

2. Cut a rectangle of paper this height. It should be wide enough to wrap all the way around the tube, plus 1"–2" extra.

3. Stick the paper to the tube in one of three ways: apply spray adhesive to the back of the paper and lightly mist the tube; line the edges on the back of the paper with double-sided tape (you may want to add a few strips of tape to the center of the paper as well); or try coating the paper with decoupage glue.

Make

Carefully stick down one vertical edge of the paper. Slowly wrap the paper around the tube, smoothing out air bubbles as you go.

Finish

Our favorite thing to do with the lid of the tube is to stick a paper or fabric flower on it. (See the Newspaper Flower and the Resplendent Rose in The Extras chapter.) If you like, cut out a circle of paper or felt to adhere to the top of the lid first (trace the lid to get the size right). Then, use hot glue to stick the felt and/or flower down.

DELTA AIR LINES
DELTA

FANCY FABRIC ENVELOPE

This decorative envelope can be made of any combinations of fabrics. Depending on what fabrics you choose, the finished envelope can be whimsical, elegant, or sophisticated. Lined with heavyweight interfacing, each envelope is pretty stiff and will keep your gift from bending. If you really want to protect your artwork/photos/documents, put a piece of lightweight cardboard in the envelope with them. (If the photos or artwork are really important, make sure the cardboard is acid-free.)

For creative reuses, these envelopes actually make a cute clutch, or if you add straps, a kid-sized messenger or tote bag.

Have

- Three fabrics that work nicely together
- Pretty button
- Heavyweight fusible interfacing (We use Pellon 808 Craft Fuse.)
- Iron
- Pencil

Optional, but Helpful

- Rotary cutter and cutting mat
- Quilter's clear grid ruler
- Math degree (kidding)

Prepare

1. Decide the size you want your finished envelope to be (for example, 8" × 11").
2. Choose which of your fabrics will be the front of the flap (A), the inside of the flap (B), and the front of the envelope (C) (figure I1).
3. To determine the size to cut pieces A and B, add 1¼" to the width, and multiply the height by 1.6, then round up to the nearest ½". For instance, if you want your final envelope to be 8" × 11", you will cut pieces A and B to 9¼" × 18".
4. To determine the size to cut piece C, add ½" to the width and 1" to the height (using the same example, you would cut piece C to 8 ½" × 12"). Iron heavyweight fusible interfacing to the back of fabric C before you cut the fabric to size.

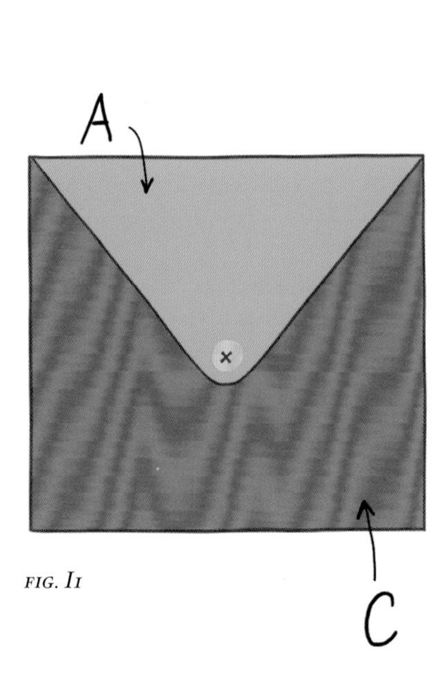

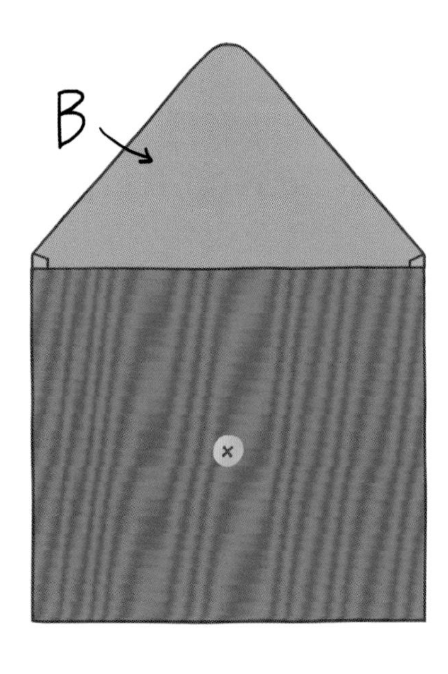

FIG. I1

Make

1. Fold the top edge of piece C toward the wrong side by ½". Iron a sharp crease. Do this once again. Sew this edge with a ¼" seam allowance. Set it aside.

2. Put pieces A and B right sides together. Take the height of your finished envelope (11" in this case) and add ¼"; measure this dimension (11¼") up from the bottom of the fabric. Draw a horizontal line across the fabric to mark this measurement (figure I2).

3. Place a mark on this line ¼" from the left and right edges of the fabric. Place a third mark on the top edge of the fabric, directly in the center (figure I3).

4. Connect these three marks to form a triangle. Round off the top corner so that it no longer meets the top edge of the fabric.

5. Draw vertical lines down the left and right sides of the fabric from your ¼" marks to the bottom (figure I4).

6. With fabrics A and B still right sides together and aligned, pin and sew along one of the vertical lines, up and around the curve of your triangle, and down the other vertical line (figure I5).

7. Trim your fabric approximately ¼" around the outside of your stitch. Cut a few notches around the curve of the triangle (being careful not to cut into your stitches).

8. Flip the sewn piece right side out, smooth out all the edges, and iron it flat.

9. Place fabric C and fabric A right sides together, making sure fabric B is turned to the back and aligning the bottom unhemmed edges (the hemmed edge of fabric C is the top edge). If one piece is slightly wider than the other, this is OK.

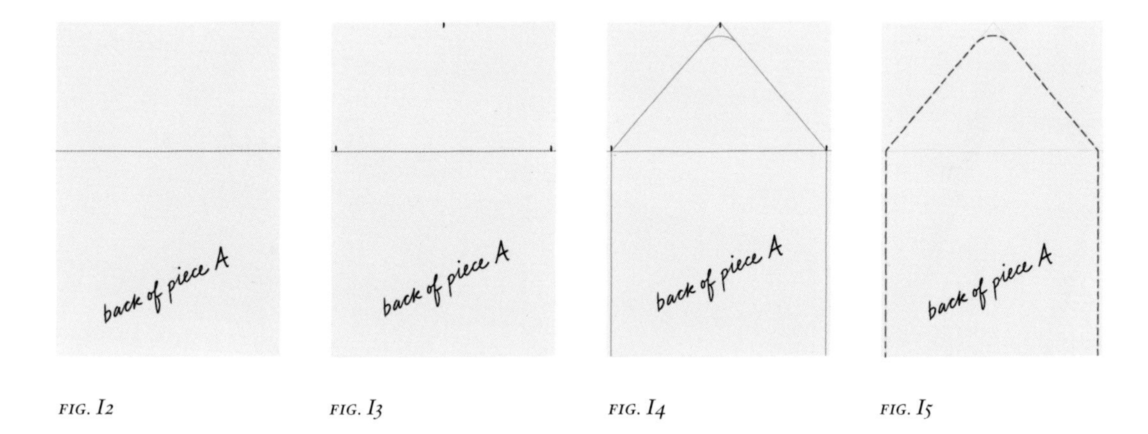

FIG. I2 *FIG. I3* *FIG. I4* *FIG. I5*

10. Stitch along the sides and bottom of fabric C with a ¼" seam allowance, leaving the top hemmed edge open. Be sure to reinforce your seams at the top so the front of the envelope doesn't pull apart with use.

11. Trim off the bottom two corners, and flip the envelope right side out. Iron it flat. The triangle will fold in at the sides a bit where it tucks into the bottom of the envelope. Just iron these folds down nicely as well.

12. Top stitch around the entire perimeter of the envelope with a ⅛" seam allowance (figure I6).

FIG. I6

Finish

1. Flip the top of the envelope down and iron a sharp crease.

2. Sew and cut a buttonhole into the tip of the triangle. Alternately, sew on a Velcro closure, and cover the front of the triangle with a sassy bow or flower from our accessories section.

Steely Dan/greatest hits
Mfd. by RCA Music Service under License
6550 East 30th Street
Indianapolis, Indiana 46219
TWINPACK
STEELY DAN
GREATEST HITS
ABC Records, Inc.
8255 Beverly Blvd., Los Angeles, California 90048
S 214341

GAME BOARD BOX

We cannot even begin to count how many amazing old games we've come across, everywhere from yard sales to thrift stores, Goodwill, flea markets, our aunt's house, and even our own basements (good grief, we're *that* old). If you're pretty sure no one's playing them anymore, or you can't find most of the pieces, the game boards themselves can be made into fantastic (and useful!) storage boxes. We particularly like colorful boards, like the old Snoopy Card Game, Monopoly, or Sorry. For a more subdued look, or a mortician friend, go with an old Ouija board.

Have

- One good game board of your choice
- Permanent marker or other writing utensil that you can see on the board
- Box cutter or a craft knife
- Tape (Decorative tape can be pretty here, but feel free to use household tape like masking, electrical, or duct tape. Use whichever will look best around the edges of your game board box.)
- Normal-sized shoe box (If you must know, I had a Rockport box. I have bad feet.)
- Straight edge or quilter's grid ruler
- Hot glue
- Acrylic medium or decoupage glue

Prepare

1. Open up the shoebox by slicing each of the four corners from the top edge to the bottom. This is your template.

2. Unfold your game board, and turn it so the fold line is horizontal. Decide whether the front or back of the game board will be the outside of your box, and have that side face up. It is your choice. I used the printed front side as the inside of my box, you might like it on the outside. Tomato, *tomahhhto*.

3. Place your box template horizontally on top of your game board, so the top horizontal fold aligns with the fold of the game board and the left flap touches the left edge of the game board (figure J1).
   TIP: Is the bottom of the box template overhanging the bottom edge of the game board? If no, perfect! If yes, measure the overhang and cut that amount off of each flap of your box template before going any further (figure J2).

4. With the template aligned according to step 3, hold steady and trace around both side flaps and the bottom flap. Do not trace the top flap yet.

5. Measure the width and height of the inside rectangle in your template (what had been the bottom of the shoe box). In my case, it was 11½" × 5½". Whatever your measurement is, add it to the top flap, extending the flap by this measurement. (That extra amount will eventually fold down and serve as your lid.) Draw the shape of the extended flap on the game board

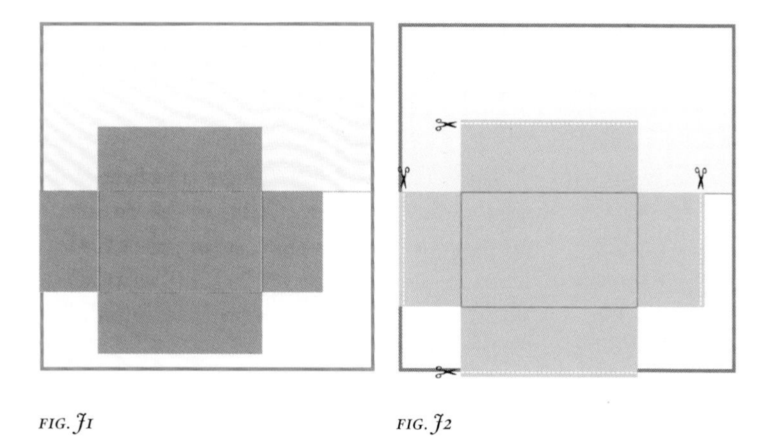

FIG. J1 *FIG. J2*

(figure J3). Make a mark where the top flap ends and your added measurement begins, so you can score and fold the top at the right place later.

6. Put your template aside, and use your box cutter or craft knife to cut your marked shape out of the game board.

7. Use your cutter and a straight edge to score (but not cut through) the central rectangle of your box and the line where the lid attaches to the top flap (figure J4).

Make

1. The easiest scenario is that your scoring will enable you to gently fold each line, and you'll watch your neato box just come together. So, flip over the board and begin to work each scored line into folded creases, folding up and inward.

2. It's possible that if your game board may be old enough to have become brittle and may actually break as you try to fold the sides into place. No worries, this is just what your hot glue gun is for! Run a bead of glue at each junction that needs to be connected, and hold them together for a few seconds until they are secure.

3. As the walls meet to become corners, connect them with a thin line of hot glue, also.

4. After each of the side walls is up, fold the lid so that it neatly falls into place over the top of the box.
NOTE: If the lid breaks as you fold it, don't use hot glue here, as it will not allow for the easy opening and closing of the lid. Your tape will come in handy here. Lay the lid right on top of the box, and run the edge of a piece of tape all the way across the edge of the lid, where the lid meets the box. Press the other edge of the tape down onto the box itself. Open the lid, see if your tape works well as a "hinge," and add another piece if necessary for added strength. Repeat the procedure on the inside of the box.

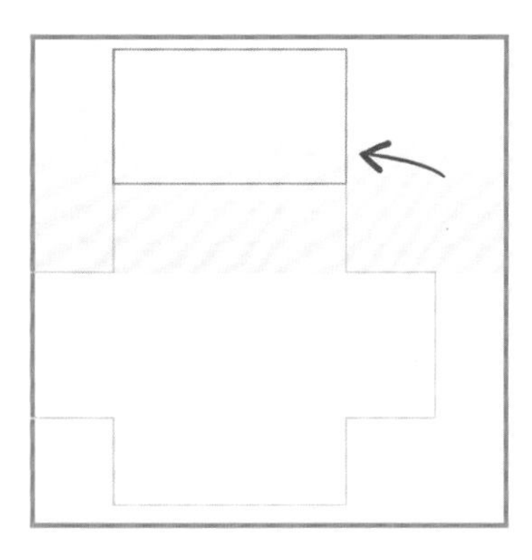

FIG. J3

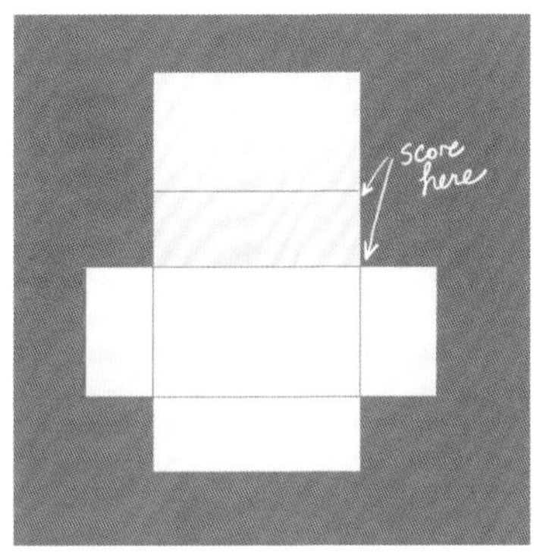

FIG. J4

Finish

1. Run decorative tape securely along each corner seam of the box, and fold over both edges. Trim the ends of the tape for neat corners. If you feel your box is a bit fragile, use a more utilitarian tape first, then cover it with decorative tape.

2. Sometimes decorative tape isn't as sticky as we might hope and will begin to peel up on the edges. Brush acrylic medium or a decoupage glue over the edges of the tape to secure it for posterity.

Try

Can pieces from the game be used decoratively on the box? Would the play money or cards fold nicely over the seams or cover an ugly spot on the box? Would a plastic piece make a perfect handle with which to open the lid? Play with it, see what you like, and then attach these fun additions with hot glue or decoupage glue.

RCA VICTOR

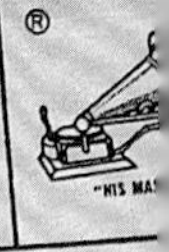

But Wait! There's More!

Another thought on packaging is to use vintage album covers in which to tuck your gifts. Who doesn't want a copy of *Saturday Night Fever* with the BeeGees in sparkling jumpsuits or Bruce's iconic jean-clad bum and red bandanna or even Debbie Gibson with her hair in scrunchies hanging on their wall? Also, if the pieces of a game are partially lost, broken, and otherwise unusable, the original game board's box itself makes a great package. ♛

SPARTUS
SPARTUS CAMERA CORP.

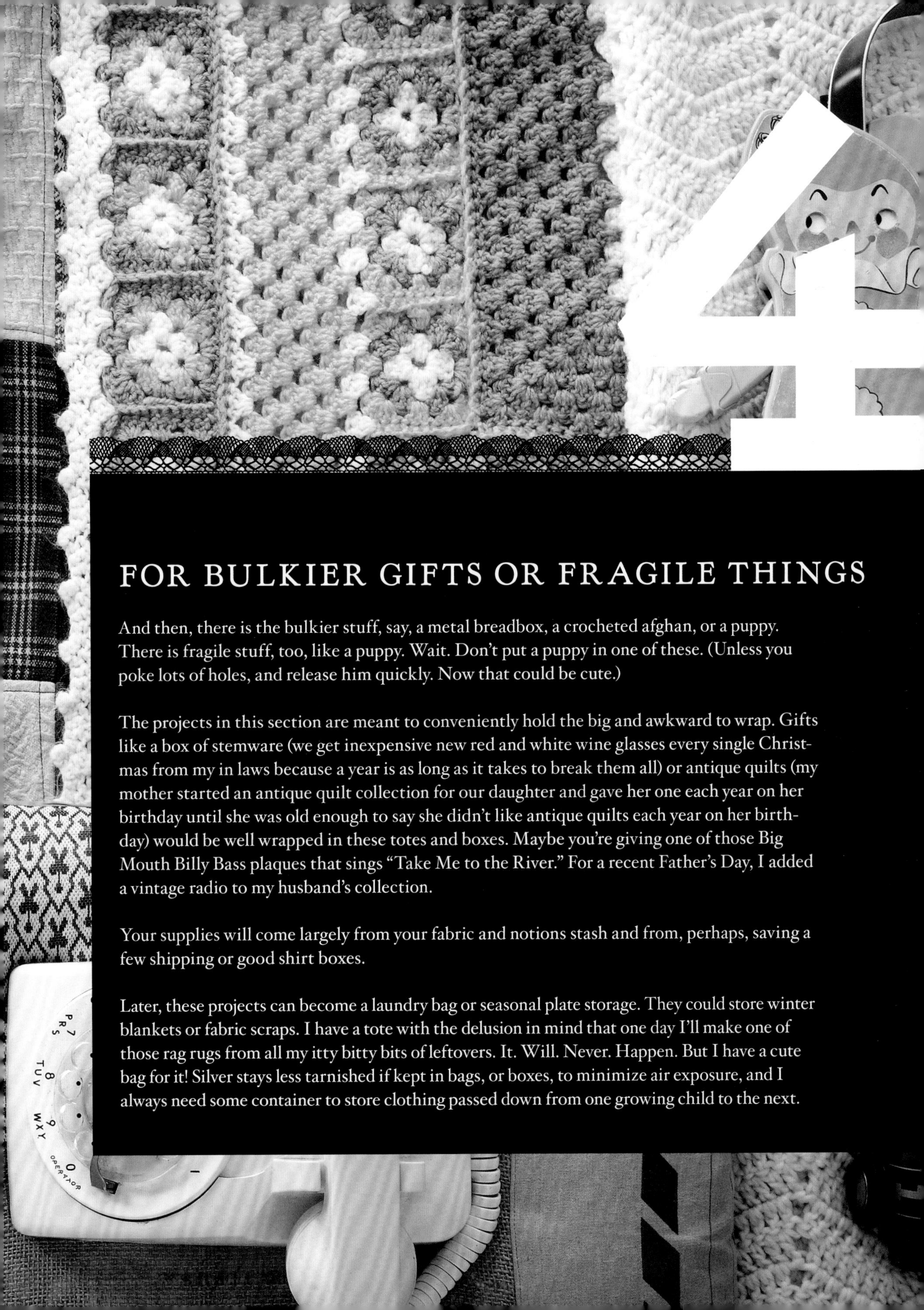

4

FOR BULKIER GIFTS OR FRAGILE THINGS

And then, there is the bulkier stuff, say, a metal breadbox, a crocheted afghan, or a puppy. There is fragile stuff, too, like a puppy. Wait. Don't put a puppy in one of these. (Unless you poke lots of holes, and release him quickly. Now that could be cute.)

The projects in this section are meant to conveniently hold the big and awkward to wrap. Gifts like a box of stemware (we get inexpensive new red and white wine glasses every single Christmas from my in laws because a year is as long as it takes to break them all) or antique quilts (my mother started an antique quilt collection for our daughter and gave her one each year on her birthday until she was old enough to say she didn't like antique quilts each year on her birthday) would be well wrapped in these totes and boxes. Maybe you're giving one of those Big Mouth Billy Bass plaques that sings "Take Me to the River." For a recent Father's Day, I added a vintage radio to my husband's collection.

Your supplies will come largely from your fabric and notions stash and from, perhaps, saving a few shipping or good shirt boxes.

Later, these projects can become a laundry bag or seasonal plate storage. They could store winter blankets or fabric scraps. I have a tote with the delusion in mind that one day I'll make one of those rag rugs from all my itty bitty bits of leftovers. It. Will. Never. Happen. But I have a cute bag for it! Silver stays less tarnished if kept in bags, or boxes, to minimize air exposure, and I always need some container to store clothing passed down from one growing child to the next.

BESPOKE TOTE

This is for the gift that actually comes in a box and needs to be given in its original box, such as a Star Wars Lego kit or fragile plate settings. It is also for the gift that needs the safety of a box, for any reason. Whatever the size of the box, this bag should fit it like a tailored suit. Going to a wedding? Make the bag out of silk taffeta or creamy wool. A housewarming barbeque? Try classic cotton seersucker. Choose the perfect fabrics, trims, and buttons to fit your recipient and occasion, and long after the wine glasses have broken, this bag will still be grabbed for quick shopping trips, books or movies for a car trip, light picnics, or a quick spend-the-night bag for children.

The very diligent Katherine Skene, of the blog *Carolyn and Me,* ran this project through the ringer for us, and gave us some great feedback. Her thoughts were:

> *I can see this being a favorite project in the book. I love the idea of making a custom bag to give a gift (especially when it's oversized!) that can be used for everyday things afterward. I added a pocket to the front of mine to include a card or note.*

Have

- Fabric for the main body of the bag
- Fabric for the straps (or heavyweight ribbon, strap webbing, or old neckties, if you want something pre-made)
- Buttons or trim, if you like
- Fabric measuring tape
- Ruler
- Straight pins
- Fusible interfacing, if you want your fabric to be more crisp and sturdy

Prepare

1. First figure out the dimensions of your fabric. To determine the width, measure your box; add the length of the side + the length of the front + 2". This will be your width (figure K1).

2. To determine the height, hold a ruler or measuring tape up to the front of your box. Decide how tall you want your bag to be. There is no right answer here, you're just using your best judgment. We found that 4" to 6" above the box makes for a nice bag height. Now, add the height of the bag + the height of the bag (again) + the length of the side + 8". This will be the height of your fabric (figure K2).

3. Cut out a piece of fabric this width and height. Depending on the fabric you've chosen, you may want to back it with fusible interfacing to give your bag a crisper, sturdy appearance. Serge or zigzag the edges (or trim them with pinking shears) to prevent fraying.

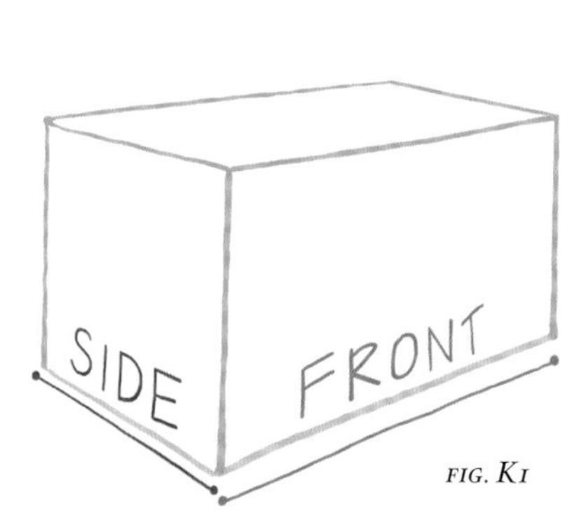

FIG. K1

FIG. K2

MAKE

1. Fold the fabric right sides together so the top edges meet. Stitch the sides with a ¼" seam allowance. Leave the sewn piece inside out.

2. From the bottom of the bag, near the corner, grab a piece of the fabric from the front and back of the bag. Pull apart these pieces, so a triangle forms at the bottom corner with the side seam running straight through the middle. Take your time so the triangle is nice and smooth (figure K3).

3. Re-measure the side of your box and add ½". Slide a ruler up and down the triangle until you find the spot where the width from one side of the triangle to the other matches that measurement. For instance, if the side of your box is 6", find the spot where the triangle is 6½" wide (figure K4).

4. Draw a pencil line here, and place a pin to hold the fabric in place. Sew across the line, reinforcing the stitches well at the beginning and end.

5. Repeat steps 2–4 with the other corner.

6. Press the vertical seams to one side, then flip the sewn piece right side out.

7. Top stitch about ⅛" along the seam from the outside of your bag, being sure to stitch through the seam allowance underneath. This topstitching will reinforce your seams and make your bag sturdier (figure K5).

8. Fold and iron the top edge of the bag under by about ½", twice, and stitch it down. Fold under and iron the top edge again, by about 3". Hold on, no stitching!

FINISH

1. Make some straps for your bag using the technique outlined in the Farmer's Daughter's Ribbon project (see page 153), or use pre-made straps or webbing, or even heavy duty ribbon if you have it. Here are some more suggestions.

   - We made each strap long enough to sew over the front and back of the bag, all the way down to the bottom edge. To do this, fold the edge of the ribbon under toward the wrong side and pin the ribbon down to the bottom edge of the front side just a few inches in from the left edge. Pin the ribbon to the front, pull out enough ribbon for a generous handle, then pin the ribbon to the opposite side of the front the same number of inches in from the right edge. Do the same on the back side. Make sure the handle lengths match up, then top stitch the ribbon to the bag.

☞ If you want your straps to be attached to the inside of the bag, pin your straps to the inside top of the bag (over your 3" fold), tuck the ends under that same fold, and sew them on as shown (figure K6).

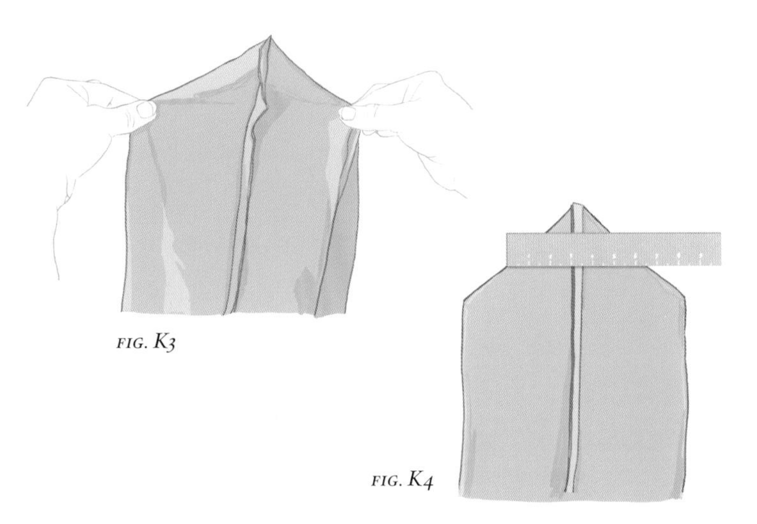

FIG. K3

FIG. K4

2. Add buttons, trim, embroidery, appliqué, or any other decoration that suits you.

FIG. K5

3. Iron a crease that connects the two bottom corners of the bag, both on the front side and on the back. Then, iron a crease from each of the bottom corners up to the top of the bag so that the bag takes on a box-like shape. You can run the very edge of the folded crease through your sewing machine, stitching as close to the edge as possible, to give the bag a crisply tailored shape.

TIP: To help the bag retain its shape, cut a piece of scrap cardboard or chipboard the size of the bottom of the bag and drop it in.

FIG. K6

1
© Ed-U-Cards
4
© Ed-U-Cards
© Ed-U-Cards
4
1
© Ed-U-Cards

IMAGINATION IS MORE IMPORTANT THAN KNOWLEDGE.

✿ ALBERT EINSTEIN ✿

SOAP OPERA BOX

We certainly don't claim to be the ones to have thought up this project. In fact, when we first decided we wanted to include it, right away I knew it had to be called the Soap Opera Box, because that's where I saw it so many times before. I grew up sneaking in episodes of *The Young and the Restless*, which my mother would watch while she folded laundry. I wasn't supposed to see them, but sometimes I could stand at the back of the room for several minutes before she'd notice and shoo me away. On the show, there was never a gift given that required the ripping of paper and tissue. All presents given *looked* like a package you would want to tear into, but instead, there was only the genteel lifting of a bow-adorned lid and the revealing of what was inside. I thought this was so glamorous. Now I see this as just a really good way to use paper—without having the paper being ripped right off and thrown away afterward. And while it may not be so glamorous as I remember, it certainly looks lovely.

Have

- Box with a lid (A shoebox is great.)
- Paper (If you have pretty wrapping paper on hand, use it now!)
- Scissors or craft knife
- Spray adhesive
- Pencil
- Straight edge

Prepare

1. Take the lid off the box. Cut the paper large enough so that while sitting under the box, each side can wrap over the top edge of the box, with a few inches to spare.

2. Place the box in the center of the wrong side of the paper.

3. Outline the edge of your box with a pencil.

4. Trim the corners as shown (figure L1). If you are a perfectionist (Hello, Melody!), you might trim these using a straight edge. (She would.)

5. Lay some newspaper or other scrap paper outside to protect the ground, and using spray adhesive, coat the wrong side of the paper you're using and lightly mist the outside of the box.

6. Very carefully, place the box in the center of the paper, aligning it with your pencil marks.

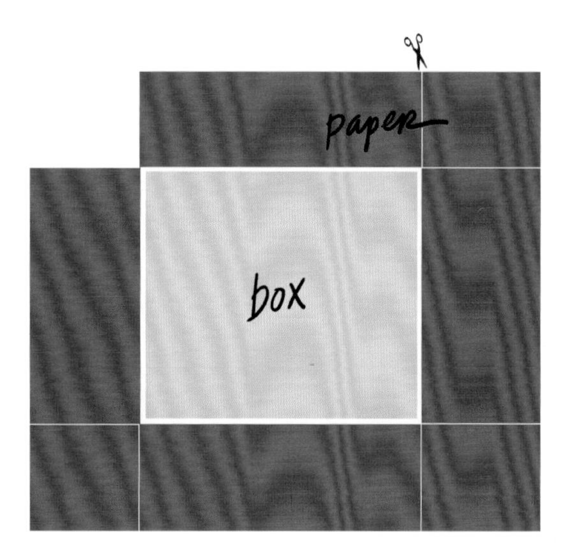

FIG. L1

Make

1. Bring the whole thing back inside.

2. Now you're going to wrap the sides of the box. The easiest way to do this is to hang one edge of the box over the edge of a table, and beginning underneath, slowly push the paper upward. Avoid air bubbles!

3. Smooth the paper over the top edge and into the inside of box. Do this for all four sides.

4. Flip over the box, and smooth the bottom, eliminating any air bubbles.

5. Repeat all steps with the lid of the box.

Finish

Wrap a ribbon around the lid of the box, and glue it on the inside of the lid. Do the same for the box itself, making sure your ribbon aligns perfectly with that of the lid. Top it off with a big bow or flower in the center. You're soap opera worthy now! Take a bow with Susan Lucci!

Try

- You can use the same technique with fabric and heavy-duty fusible web. Use a hot iron to adhere the fabric to the box.
- And don't forget about wallpaper (especially our favorite: vintage). Last year, we sold a roll of early '80s Smurf wallpaper, from a little flea market booth we have. It would have made an excellent, and unforgettable, package!

THE MELODY-DIDN'T-MEAN-TO-MAKE-IT TOTE

This gift-wrapping option really was an accidental project. Melody was working on an alternate version of another project from this book—and the whole experiment was going terribly—when she unexpectedly came up with this tote. We really liked it, but what would we use it for? We hemmed and hawed, and *poof*, we figured it out. This bag is perfect for giving a rolled-up quilt or afghan, or a set of towels rolled up with washcloths on top—something many newlyweds or new homeowners want. *I* want new towels, and I'm neither newly wedded nor in a new home.

This tote is also really nice for baby diapers, cloth or disposable. When I was having my third and then fourth babies, all we really needed was a stash of diapers. After using the diapers, I would have kept this tote to save those rapidly outgrown little clothes that are special and make me cry when I think of losing them. As of now, I have three or four really tacky gift bags filled to the top with newborn booties, gowns, and onesies. (Don't tell Melody I said that.)

When our intrepid tester Brittney Anderson, of the blog *Brittney Anderson*, took a whack at it, she thought of still more uses:

> *I might make it a little bit smaller to accommodate a wine bottle, and instead of (or in addition to) batting, use insulator to keep the wine chilled [Allison's fave idea yet]. Or keep it the same size and add in some cute dishtowels or napkins for a great hostess gift. I also think it would make a cute picnic pouch—you can fit your lunch, plates, and utensils inside, and it would be really cute in a gingham fabric. Again, lining in oilcloth would make it extra useful in this department [the tote would then be virtually waterproof, and easily wiped]. I made mine in a shiny fabric I had on hand, making it perfect for fancy gift giving, but in another fabric it could be perfect for giving and storing toys. It's tall enough to fit a handful of small dolls, and think of all the Lego bricks you could stuff in there!*

These instructions make a bag that is approximately 10" × 18". To make a different size, adjust the diameter of the bottom and the height of the fabric accordingly (add 3" to your final desired height). As for the width of the fabric, you just need to cut it wide enough to reach all the way around your circle, and then some.

Have

- Fabric for the outside of the bag (hereby known as fabric A): one scrap piece larger than 11" × 11" (this will be the bottom of the bag) and another cut to 35" × 21". NOTE: For our bags, we stitched two pieces of fabric together to make this size. The top 6" of our bag is a contrasting fabric. We even used silk. We're so fancy that way.
- Fabric for the inside of the bag (hereby known as fabric B): one scrap piece larger than 11" × 11" (this will be the bottom of the lining) and another cut to 35" × 21"
- Quilt batting: one piece 35" × 14"; one piece larger than 11" × 11" (This will line the bottom of the bag.)
- Ribbon
- Straight pins
- Compass

Prepare

1. Use a compass to draw a circle 10½" in diameter on a piece of paper. Cut this circle out to use as a pattern piece. (Our pattern tester, Brittney, traced a 10½" pot lid. So clever!)

2. Stack the scrap quilt batting on the wrong side of your smaller scrap piece of fabric A. Hand or machine quilt the pieces together according to the instructions on your quilt batting (some battings call for rows of stitches at least 3" apart, some larger). Your quilting can be anything from a few simple rows to a free-motion quilting pattern. On one of our bags, we stitched a flower shape here. (Note: We used fusible batting and first ironed it down to the fabric using a sheet of parchment to keep it from sticking to the iron.)

3. Trace and cut out your circle from quilted fabric A, and then trace and cut out the circle from the smaller piece of fabric B.

4. Iron or pin down the 35" × 14" batting to the bottom portion of 35" × 21" fabric A. (The top portion of the fabric will be unlined and gathered to close the bag.) Quilt the batting to the fabric using the same recommendations in step 2 (figure M1).

Make

1. Now we're going to stitch the side wall to the bottom circle of the bag. In making this project, we realized it can be tricky to get the length of the fabric just right so it goes all the way around the circle without buckling or gathering. This technique will help you get the length just right. You may find it helpful to read through the steps once before starting.

2. Turn fabric A so that the batting is on your right and running vertically down the right side of the piece and facing up; the plain fabric side is on your left. Using a ruler, make a dark horizontal pencil line about an inch from the top of the rectangle (figure M2).

3. Fold the top edge of the rectangle down on that line, and place a noticeable pencil mark on the right folded edge of the rectangle. We'll call this point A (figure M3).

4. Leave the fabric folded, and put that same edge of the rectangle, right sides together, against the edge of the circle. Set your machine at the widest basting stitch, and using a ¼" seam allowance, begin stitching at point A (figure M4). Stitch the first 3" or so of the rectangle to the edge of the circle, turning the fabric constantly to stay aligned with the circle edge.

5. After the first 3" are sewn, adjust your machine to your usual stitch width. Continue sewing around the circle. Go slowly, being careful to keep the two edges nicely aligned.

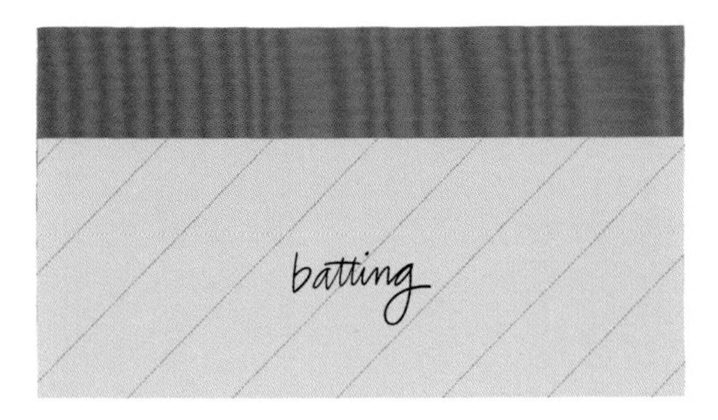

FIG. M1

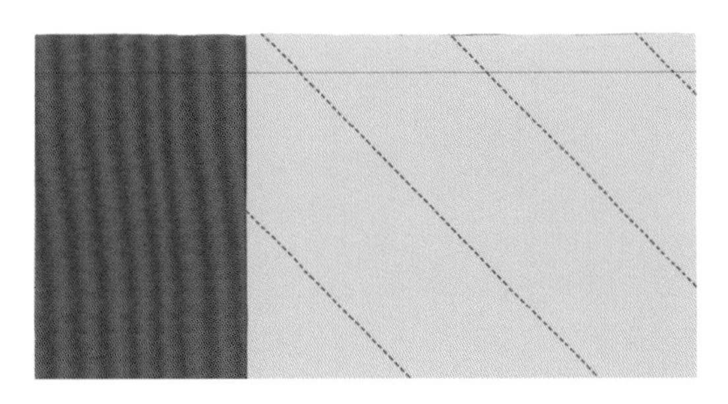

FIG. M2

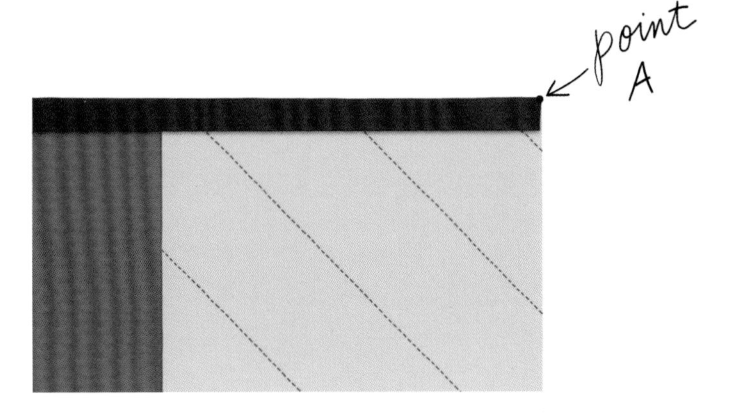

FIG. M3

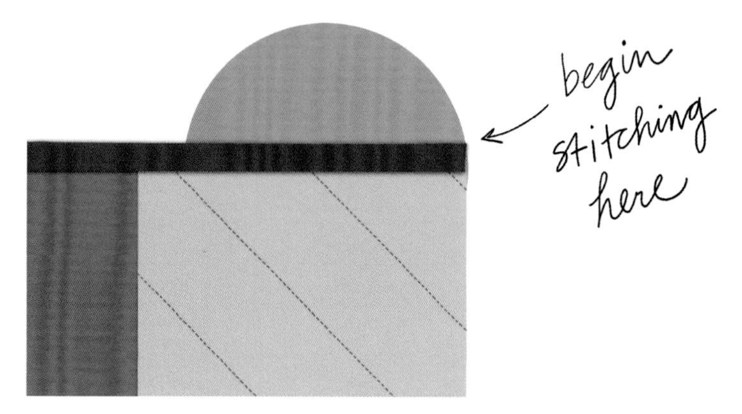

FIG. M4

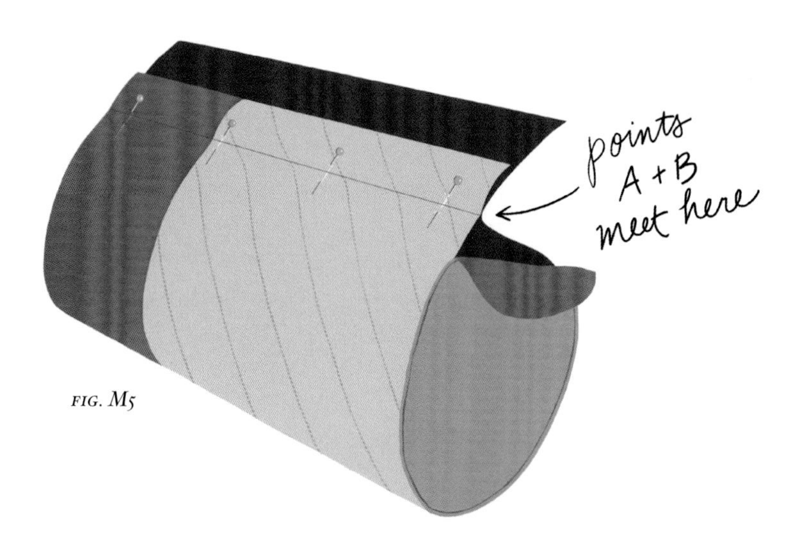

FIG. M5

FIG. M6

6. As you near the spot where you began (point A), reset your machine to the wide basting stitch. Finish the last few inches of the circle with this stitch until you reach point A.

7. The spot where your rectangle meets point A will be called point B. Place a pencil mark at point B on your rectangle.

8. Now, pick out the basting stitches and pull the two ends of your rectangle up away from the circle. We're going to take a quick break from the circle and sew the side wall of the bag.

9. Unfold the edge by point A. The place where points A and B meet is where you will sew the wall of your bag. Pin the two sides of the rectangle together, right sides facing, with everything aligned (neither side of the rectangle should be askew); points A and B should be perfectly overlapped. If you pin your fabric exactly where points A and B overlap, you will have a perfectly fitted wall for your cylinder (figure M5).

10. Stitch along the pencil line you previously drew in step 2. Be sure to set your stitch length back to normal first! Cut off any excess fabric.

11. Now that your wall is sewn, you can complete the bottom edge. Begin stitching where you left off on the side of the circle. When you stitch over your seams (from the wall of the cylinder), just stitch them to one side.

12. To help the sides of the bag curve nicely, and the bottom to lay flat, clip notches all the way around the edge of your circle, outside the seam you just finished sewing. Do not clip into the seam.

OPTIONAL: Push the vertical side seams to one side. Then from the outside of the bag, top stitch along the vertical side seam, about ⅛" away from the original seam. Be sure to top stitch through the seam allowance underneath. This topstitching will reinforce your seam and make your bag sturdier (figure M6).

13. Repeat steps 1–11 for fabric B (disregarding the batting).

14. Fold and iron the raw edge of fabric A toward the wrong side by ¾". Fold and iron the edge of fabric B toward the wrong side by 1".

15. Sew and cut two vertical buttonholes side by side on the front of fabric A where you want the top to cinch together. We sewed ours approximately 2" from the top edge.

16. Drop fabric B into fabric A, wrong sides together, to create the lining. All of the seams should be hidden at this point. Line up the top folded edges of A and B, and sew all the way around, as close to the edge as possible.

17. Sew two seams all the way around the bag to create a channel for the ribbon. One seam should be above the buttonhole, and the other will be below. Make sure the channel is wide enough to accommodate your ribbon.

18. Attach a safety pin to the end of the ribbon and run it through the channel you just created. It should go in one buttonhole and out the other.

19. Have a drink. You've earned it!

But Wait! There's More!

When giving bulky gifts, we also like to find old hard suitcases of varying sizes and put the gifts in them. These suitcases make the ultimate gift around a gift, and often only costs a couple of dollars at thrift stores or flea markets. Melody has used spray paint to put stripes or patterns on them, and they are adorable. Elsie Larson and Rachel Denbow of the beloved Red Velvet Shop worked up another great idea that we love: they covered the front and back of a suitcase with fabric! Scrumptious! My husband uses one of those '70s hard case *Rockford Files*-esque briefcases to carry his laptop. I keep a travel/train case, the kind brides in the '60s purchased for their honeymoons, on the vanity of our children's bathroom. It is great medicine storage. It even has a lock and key. ♛

5

WHEN YOUR GIFT IS EDIBLE, DRINKABLE, OR GROWABLE

Sometimes, the very best presents are scrumptiously consumable: loose herbal teas, infused oils, crisp pinot grigios, or a chocolately shiraz. Maybe a heart-and-tummy-warming casserole of baked cheese grits. Sometimes, a gift is something to be grown and nurtured (but fortunately not into something that can talk back). Give a small spathiphyllum, lemony basil, or bright orange Gerber daisies. Dried herbs from your garden, fresh roasted coffee beans. Melody said something about maté tea, but I have no idea *what* that is. Does Lipton make it?

With the following packages, you can give the gift of eating, drinking, or growing in a lovely container that can be used and used again. The best part? These thoughtful gifts are doable on nearly any budget. Give homemade candies, herbal throat lozenges (Really! I received some once, thanks Margo!), or those cookie/cake recipes that layer in a jar.

Materials here will be recycled glass bottles, jars, or cookie tins, and your fabric and notions stash again. For the glass, you'll need some spray paint in various colors. We tend to keep paint around; for a few dollars a can, it is great to have on hand.

The painted jars and bottles are fantastic when used later for bud vases or a sprig of fall leaves. A smaller vessel can be continually refilled with olive oil or balsamic vinegar. These painted jars and bottles hold our children's messy paint water, and if you have several as a grouping, they are beautiful on a mantle or table, as a *tableau* (fancy, right?). This spring, being that I live in Georgia, I dried some dogwood blossoms (my favorite) with Borax and did this very thing on our dining room table.

The casserole cover can be reused with the same casserole, or used on its own to serve fresh baked goods. It will make a sweet carrier for muffins, bagels, or that crazy gooey monkey bread stuff. (Just wrap that in plastic wrap first to keep the goo off the fabric.) And naturally, when you make a tea towel to wrap a bottle of wine or oil, you then have, well, a tea towel!

CA REDEMPTION
RUM

PAINT IT

You'd be hard pressed to find a much simpler project than this one and yet have it end up looking so beautiful! There is no sewing involved, and one good hour, maybe an hour and a half, in a well-ventilated place will allow you to layer several coats of paint for a fine, even, drip-free finish. This is the trick: spray each coat lightly, and take the time to let each coat dry before the next. Think good pedicure. If you slop several layers on, you'll have those smudges and scratches in the end. Don't rush the putting on of your shoes!

While it takes only a little time to get a nice coat of paint on the glass, prepping it can take a total of a few hours. This process is best done some day when you have a little time to get these bottles and jars ready before you need to paint them. One idea is to run a few jars through the dishwasher one night as you are going to bed, then soak them while you have coffee and breakfast, and then later in the day, use your adhesive remover for the final smooth. The finished pieces look aMAYzing with just a clutch of wild flowers or even inexpensive carnations from the grocery store floral shop.

The things to collect here include recycled glass vessels with potential. We used pasta sauce jars, soda bottles (Brown's Cream Soda is great), and queso, pickle, peanut butter, and jelly jars. A couple of vessels we found especially nice were a tall rum bottle and a very narrow bottle of Americanized absinthe. What?

Have

- Any glass jar, bottle, or vessel
- Spray paint, any colors you like, matte or gloss (Matte paint works equally as well as gloss, it just produces a different result. Also, the gloss seems to retain some stickiness longer. No, we don't know why.)
- A place to spray paint without passing out, and some old newspaper or a piece of old board you don't mind getting really colorful
- Adhesive remover, like Goo Gone, rubbing alcohol, or nail polish remover and a rough rag
- 120-grit sandpaper, for stubborn adhesive and bits of label

Prepare

1. Run your containers through the dishwashing machine once, and a lot of the label and adhesive will just wash away. To get rid of what is left, soak the containers in a sink full of warm water and a splash of liquid detergent for a couple of hours.
2. Allow the containers to dry on an old towel, and then go after the remaining bits of sticky and paper with an adhesive remover and a rough rag. If you have something really stubborn, a little sandpaper should finish it off.

   TIP: Be on the lookout for a very small, black ink, UPC-like label on some jars and bottles. It will not come off with washing, but it will come off with adhesive remover. Just make sure you get it off; otherwise, when it gets hit with the first coat of paint, the ink will run thickly down the jar. It's easy to cover the mess with dark colors—not so easy with lavender or cream.

Make

1. Set up your papers or old board in a well-ventilated area. Place one vessel out, and choose a color.

2. If you plan on putting food or drink in your container when you're finished, do one of two things. Either turn it upside down to keep the paint out of the interior, or if it will not balance that way, stuff it to the rim with tissue, newspaper, or cotton balls.

3. Cover the vessel very lightly with the first coat, and let it dry for at least 15 minutes. Having a fan set up will speed the process, but don't rush it.

Finish

1. Repeat one, two, or three more times, depending on the finish that you want. Depending on the color of paint, you may need lots of coats, or just a few. Allow the paint to dry for an hour or so more. There. Be-A-YOO-tiful.

   TIP: Once your jars and bottles are done, don't run them through the dishwasher; just rinse them with soapy warm water, and if necessary, clean them out with a bottle brush, like any that would come from a grocery or home store.

Try

- Embellish your bottle: Tie some ribbon around your bottle or jar, stick on a hand-drawn label, or add one of the accessories from The Extras chapter (we highly recommend the flowers or any of our garland ideas).
- Another good candidate for this idea is one of those sad-looking tins you get at the office White Elephant Christmas/Hanukah/Kwanza/Yom Kippur/Celebrate-Everybody's-Birthday-At-Once parties that hold multiple levels of crackers or cookies. You can spray paint these as well.

hello darling

PERFECT WINE WRAP

I made this project perfect. Now, don't get me wrong. Melody is amazing and has thought of and created almost every one of these ideas. But once or twice, I come in with a stroke of genius, and WHAM. It. Is. So. Good! Which I have to say, because it is really my only contribution to the projects themselves, and of course, I could not do this if Mel had not set me up with such a brilliant idea to begin with, but still, once in a long while, it happens: I. Am. On. Fire!

We are so proud of this Perfect Wine Wrap. Not only is it the cutest presentation of a wine bottle we've ever seen, it is a most lovely and charming tea towel, besides. This project couldn't be quicker or easier, and as far as useful goes, we've outdone ourselves.

To make this, you're going to need two pieces of fabric, and we recommend that you choose something reasonably absorbent. Wanna know what we love best? Vintage towels right from the thrift store. They get a whole new life here. Paired with an Echino fabric—or any other favorite print—they couldn't look better. Other great fabrics here are linen, and naturally, 100 percent cotton. Also, anything by Melody Miller. I'm just saying. But what did *I* do to make this irresistible? I added the second piece of ribbon to seal the deal! Melody was just standing there, asking me, begging me, "What do we do with the bottom?" Two more seconds, and Melody would have come up with it, but I did it first. (I win, Mel!)

Have

- Two coordinating pieces of fabric cut to 16" × 19" (If you have another size in mind, go for it!)
- Two pieces of ribbon approximately ½"–1" wide and 24" or longer.
- Straight pins

Make

1. Pin your two fabrics right sides together. Use pins or chalk to mark the openings where you will not want to stitch. There should be a 1" opening on the left and right sides, about 2" from the top edge, and a 6" opening across the bottom (figure O1).
2. Stitch around all four sides with a ½" seam allowance. Don't sew over your marked openings!
   TIP: If you're sewing terry cloth here, we found that it works best to sew with the terry cloth on the bottom. Ours tended to stretch when we had it on top.
3. Turn the towel inside out through the 6" opening. Use a chopstick or knitting needle to poke the corners out. If necessary, iron around the edges to make

FIG. O1

FIG. O2

the seams nice and flat. Be sure that the fabric at your openings is turned inward.

4. Sew around the perimeter of the towel with a ⅛" seam allowance. Skip over the two 1" openings again, but sew straight over the 6" opening at the bottom.

5. Sew two horizontal seams directly across the towel, one above the 1" opening, and one below. This will create the channel that your ribbon will run through (figure O2).

6. Attach a safety pin to the end of your ribbon and work it through the channel.

Finish

1. Now wrap your bottle. Lay the bottle with the neck slightly overlapping the channel where the ribbon is. Starting at one side, roll the bottle and fabric all the way to the other side.

2. Pull the ribbon upward from each end to gather the towel around the neck of the bottle. Tie in a pretty bow. Tie a second piece of ribbon below the bottom of the bottle. Voilà! Best wine wrap ever!

3. To hang the towel wrapper in the kitchen, pull the ribbon until the towel gathers, and tie the ribbon in a bow. This gift can hang on a hook or door knob, or you can just tie it onto the handle of the fridge or dishwasher. It could also tie on a belt loop, so you can wipe your hands quickly and easily while you work.

NOTHING WOULD BE MORE TIRESOME THAN EATING AND DRINKING IF GOD HAD NOT MADE THEM A PLEASURE AS WELL AS A NECESSITY.

✿ VOLTAIRE ✿

LONDON
MADE IN U.S.A.
ffrr
full frequency
range recording
40058-B
(Album LGF-19)
(4 Sides)
No. 4
POLOVTSIAN DANCES
(from "Prince Igor") (Borodin-arr. Rimsky-Korsakov)
THE LONDON PHILHARMONIC
ORCHESTRA—Conductor:
GREGOR FITELBERG
(ARF-10235)
UNAUTHORIZED PUBLIC PERFORMANCE, BROADCASTING

LONDON
MADE IN U.S.A.
40076-A
(Album LGF-24)
(4 Sides)
No. 1
Recorded at The
Kingsway Hall,
London
(Luigini)
Conductor:
STANFORD ROBINSON
(ARF-10202)
LONDON
MADE IN U.S.A.
ffrr
full frequency
range recording
BALLET EGYPTIEN—SUITE
Allegretto (Luigini)
THE B.B.C. THEATRE ORCHESTRA
Conductor:
STANFORD ROBINSON
(ARF-10203)

JAIMIE'S CASSEROLE COVER

A fantastic hot dish can be the greatest, most welcome gift. So very many times, food is the dearest friend—when there is a new baby in the house, or when it's the house that's new. Hot dishes are especially helpful when someone has been ill or is dealing with illness. I had a car accident a couple of years ago, and sweet, angelic people (Hi, Church of the Redeemer, Atlanta!) brought meals for a month. It was edible, finger-licking love, I tell you.

When you'd like to give the gift of food, turn to this project—you not only give a hot dish, but also a dish in a pretty casserole, wrapped up like a present. When this little wrap is complete, your casserole should fit neatly inside, and the ribbon will cinch up the top of the casserole cover and tie into a big pretty bow. Each cover is to be made specifically for the casserole you choose. We love including an actual casserole as part of the gift, but if you just want to bake something and put it in a plastic container, do it. We know no one who turns down a wonderful meal just because the dish is not vintage glass.

At least half the credit for this project goes to the indomitable Jaimie Harris of *This is J*. Those long hours at Surtex in neighboring booths led to fantastic conversations and inspiration for this book. Thank you, Jaimie!

Reuses of this casserole cover are pretty easy. The cover can be reused with the same casserole or on its own to serve fresh baked goods. It will make a sweet carrier for muffins, bagels, or sticky buns. (Just wrap any gooey treats in plastic or parchment paper first to keep the sticky stuff off the fabric.)

Have

- Large piece of paper (Newspaper works fine here, butcher paper is good, too.)
- Dish to give (We love vintage Pyrex with a glass cover, but a plastic dish with a lid will do well here, too.)
- Two pieces of fabric that work nicely together
- Cotton quilt batting or Insul-Bright (if you want the cover to hold in the heat from your dish)
- Ribbon (at least ¾" wide and long enough to wrap around the top of your dish and tie in a bow)
- Scissors
- Straight pins

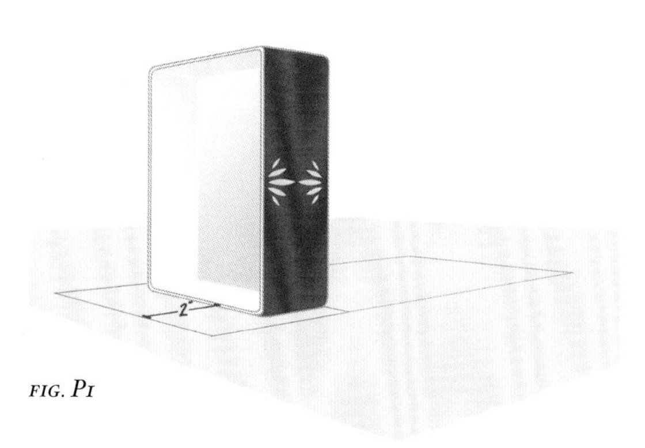

FIG. P1

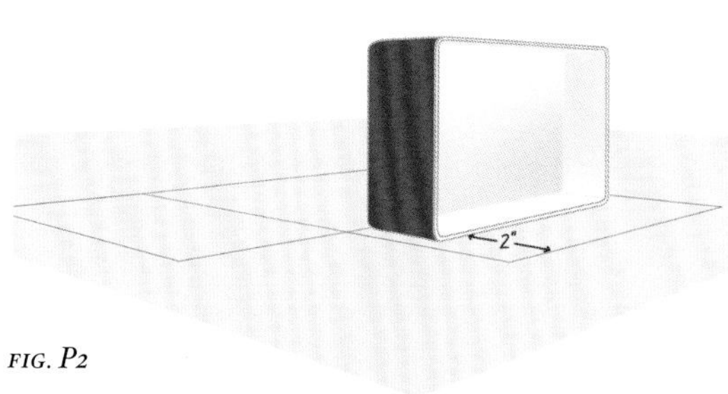

FIG. P2

PREPARE

THE PATTERN

1. Place the dish on the center of the paper, and trace a rectangle approximately ½" outside the bottom of the dish.

2. Turn the dish on its left side with the bottom edge of the dish aligned with the left side of the rectangular tracing you just made.

3. Trace ½" outside the two short sides of the dish (connecting them to the corners of the rectangle), but extend the long side out 2" beyond the long edge of the dish (figure P1).

4. Now turn the dish on its long side, aligning the bottom edge of the dish with the bottom edge of your rectangle. Trace the long side the same as the short side in step 3 (figure P2).

5. Repeat steps 3 and 4 for the other two sides of the dish. Cut out this final shape. Your finished pattern piece should look something like figure P3. Or, if the sides of the dish are more of a trapezoid shape, it may look like figure P4.

THE MATERIALS

1. Choose your fabrics for the outside and the inside of the cover. They need to be larger than the pattern piece. Press out the wrinkles.

2. Find a piece of quilt batting that is also larger than your pattern piece. Cotton works best, as polyester may get caught in your machine's feed dogs.
   OPTIONAL: Use two layers of batting for an extra-puffy cover, or Insul-Bright, which is designed to hold the heat in really well.

FIG. P3

FIG. P4

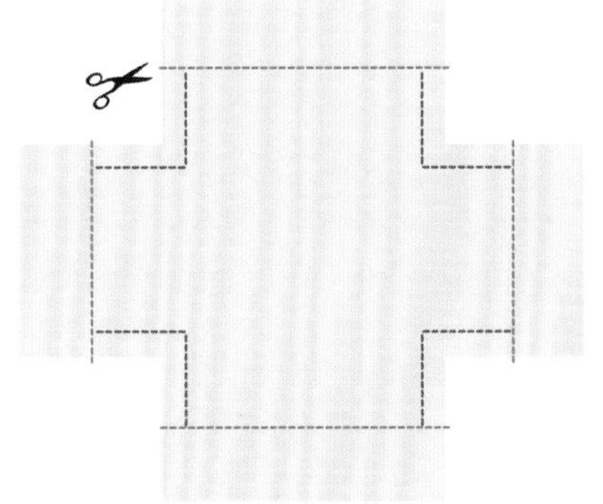

FIG. P5

3. Stack the fabrics right sides together on top of your quilt batting, and trace your pattern onto the top of the stack. Cut the fabric and batting on your traced lines.

4. Trim the ends of your quilt batting back by about 1½" (see the orange lines on figure P5). Trim all the remaining edges by about ½" (see the blue lines). These cuts don't have to be perfect (they won't show), but they will allow your batting to fit neatly into your cover (figure P5).

Make

OUTSIDE COVER

1. Center the batting on the wrong side of the outside cover fabric piece and quilt according to the instructions on your quilt batting (some batting calls for stitches at least 3" apart, some can be 8" or 12"). This quilting will keep the batting from slipping inside your casserole cover and can be anything from a few simple rows to a free-motion quilting pattern.

2. Take a look at your fabric piece. The four sides are meant to stand up and meet to form four walls. With the fabric right side up, begin standing up the edges and pinning the fabric right sides together according to figure P6. You will pin side A with side A, B with B, and so on. It may help to pin and sew one side at a time. For three of the sides, sew from the top edge down to the corner with a ¼" seam allowance. On the last side, do the same but leave the top 1½" open. This is where you will eventually insert your ribbon (figure P6). (If you're Mel, you'll sew that last side all the way up to the top anyway and will then have to pick out your stitches later.)

3. On the 1½" edge that you just left open (or picked back open), fold and iron the fabric back by ¼", so that it makes a clean opening. Neatly stitch the fabric down where you folded it back (figure P7).

4. Now iron the top edge of the cover toward the wrong side of the fabric ½" all the way around to form a sharp crease.

INSIDE COVER

1. Press the other piece of fabric for the inside cover. Repeat step 2 from the Outside Cover, except don't leave the 1½" opening. Sew all four sides all the way to the top edge of the fabric.

2. Fold and iron the top edge of the fabric toward the wrong side by ¾".

FINISH

1. Place the inside piece you've created into the outside piece, wrong sides together with the corners meeting, align the top edges, and pin them to hold everything in place. Stitch all the way around the top edge with a ⅛" seam allowance. For the open corner, allow the two open pieces to meet at the corner, and stitch over the top edge of these also.

2. Sew one more seam all the way around the top edge with a 1" seam allowance. This will create the channel for your ribbon. If your ribbon is wider than 1", you may want to make this channel wider as well.

3. Attach a safety pin to one end of your ribbon and work it all the way through the channel, starting and ending at your open corner.

4. Put your covered casserole inside, cinch the ribbon, and tie it up pretty!

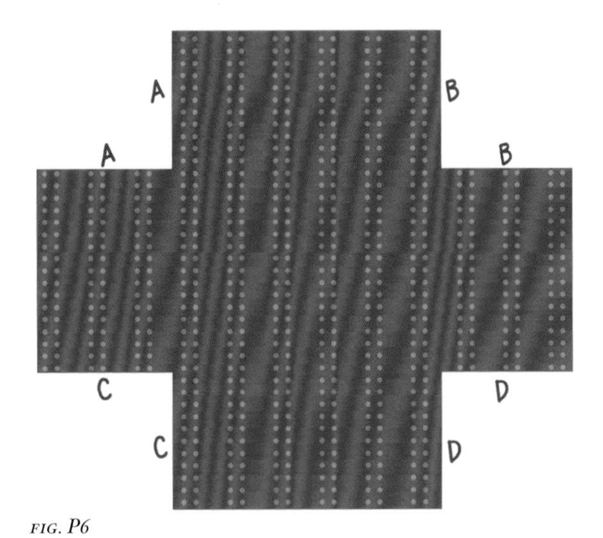

FIG. P6

FIG. P7

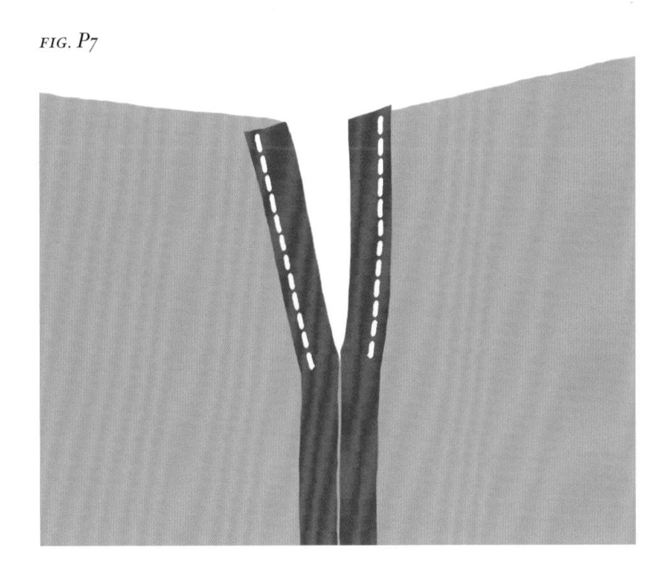

RUBY STAR'S CHEESE GRITS

If you want to give a round casserole, as shown here, you can present it in the Melody-Didn't-Mean-to-Make-It Tote on page 81 and adjust the measurements accordingly.

START WITH:

- 6 cups boiling water
- 1½ cups grits (We use Quaker Quick or Aunt Jemima Quick.)

Follow the instructions on the box for cooking the grits. Then add the good stuff.

STIR IN:

- 1½ sticks margarine or butter, your preference
- 1 pound Velveeta cheese (Yes, Velveeta. Get over it. If you are utterly opposed, use an equal amount of grated cheddar cheese, but don't expect the same smooth melting.)
- 3 eggs, beaten
- 1 teaspoon salt
- 2 teaspoons All Seasons salt
- Few drops Tabasco sauce

Pour into a buttered or sprayed casserole, and bake at 350 degrees for about one hour, or until hot and bubbly. You're welcome.

PYREX

ALLISON'S FAVORITE OATMEAL CHOCOLATE CHIP COOKIES

This recipe is from Glowly Lierman. I've known her since her husband and my dad flew planes together in the Vietnam War. Her name is actually Gloria, but when I was just two, I could only say "Glowly." My mother's recipe, which she used to make for me when I was a girl, includes this note: "Omit the chocolate chips, add coconut, and less pecans." You can follow this note or make them as shown. Today, these are my favorite, just as they were originally supposed to be, because they are *good.*

CREAM TOGETHER:

- 1 cup shortening
- 1 cup dark brown sugar
- 1 cup white sugar

ADD TO THIS MIXTURE AND BEAT:

- 2 eggs, beaten
- 2 tablespoons of water
- 1 teaspoon vanilla

MIX IN:

- 2 cups self-rising flour
- 2 cups oatmeal

THEN STIR IN:

- 6 ounces chocolate chips
- 1 cup chopped pecans

Drop by rounded spoonfuls onto a greased baking sheet, and bake at 350 degrees for about 10 minutes or until golden brown.

Bake them all at once and share, or roll extra dough into a tube shape, wrap it with plastic wrap, and store it in the freezer for instant slice and bake cookies another time.

Hint: These are wonderful to pull out of your freezer at the last minute if your house is on the market. It makes your entire home smell yummy and inviting to lookers. Also awesome for a quick sugar sacrifice to cranky kids in those hours between midafternoon and dinner.

But Wait! There's More!

We also love the idea of using a tea cup and its saucer in which to give a small plant or herb for the kitchen. Just be sure to use succulents that don't need much watering or add a thin layer of tiny gravel beneath the soil to prevent root rot.

You could decorate a vintage dish with ceramic paint pens to hold a batch of my (will be your) favorite oatmeal chocolate chip cookies. The paint pens become impermeable when directions are followed to bake the plates, or whatever ceramics you are using, in the oven.

HUGHES
PHARMACY
ASPIRIN
HANDMADE IN ENGLAND BY MONKEYPUZZLE
NOT SUITABLE FOR SMALL CHILDREN

6

FOR COLLECTIONS, SUPPLIES, OR THE ODDLY SHAPED GIFT

In an ideal world, I would have a container for everything, and each of those everythings would be in its correct container. All of my favorite pens? One lovely can. My grandmother's vintage ivory buttons? One charming box. My daily must-haves—the lip gloss, cell phone, hair elastic, Taser . . . (just kidding)? Well, this is one area that I've pulled together and truly enjoy. I carry all of these essentials about in peppy little work aprons with a comely sash. Melody made them for me, and they make up a huge part of my daily, albeit nerdy, uniform. But trust me, these aprons are much more acceptable than my around-the-house uniform of the mid-'90s: the denim, wide legged overalls, with clunky clog mules. Yes, I'm embarrassed now.

While it may sound like you should just make these projects for your own use (and you certainly should!), they are also great for gift giving, particularly when those gifts are many and small. We have children who love little things: metal cars, plastic dinosaurs, Slinkys, and marbles; fingernail polish, hair accessories, glittery sweet lip balms, Matryoshka dolls, and Japanese tape. We also have friends who love collecting small objects: vintage medicine tins, retro dice, or tiny salt-and-pepper shakers. From Christmas ornaments and unique wine bottle stoppers to the neat vintage trims and Bakelite buttons that I know Melody loves, these little containers are perfect for little things. These projects are some of the simplest in the bunch, one of which might take only five minutes. Really. Scrap fabric is again your go-to here, as well as any sorts of embellishments from your stash.

These packages can be used later in the same fashion they were given: to hold and store the original gift. Or they can be used to take lunches to work or school, the Snack Sack being an obvious holder of a sandwich, pretzels, Doritos, or gumdrops. They'll keep an iPod or smart phone cozy, too. The 5-minute Party Pouches are great for jewelry storage or travel. I keep some earplugs in one (my kids are loud, and husband snores) so the dog can't eat them. I know. Earplugs are a really dumb food choice, but he just can't resist. The Takeout Boxes can hold and store anything that needs a place to call its own: sewing notions, felt balls, math manipulatives. Clean up your space and show off your taste at the same time.

seuls
race
grâce
oeillets
parc où,
de bonne
de leur
siècles

RUBY STAR'S CHINESE TAKEOUT BOX

The Takeout Box is apparently so delightful that it up-and-disappeared from my house. Its abductor: a wonderful older lady who helps me get the nastiest dark corners of my house cleaned out every five or six weeks. I had gone out of town, left her a key, and propped her payment against a sweet little houseplant that I had dropped into one of our mock-up boxes. When I returned, my kitchen plant was gone, along with her check, and a note was left in place thanking me profusely for my kindness. It just looked like a present, but it was my plant! I didn't really mind. It was nice confirmation that Melody and I were onto a good idea. And that lady deserved at least a pretty plant for being willing to enter our home full of boys without a hazmat suit.

Have

- Fabric
- Heavyweight fusible interfacing (We use Pellon #808 Craft Fuse.)
- Sharp scissors
- Hot glue gun
- Iron
- Takeout Box template (page 182)

Optional, but Helpful

- Craft knife
- Cutting mat

Prepare

1. Copy or print out the template, and cut on the solid lines.
2. Iron the heavyweight interfacing to the back of a piece of fabric larger than your template.

Make

1. Ignoring the dashed lines, trace the outside edges of the template onto your fabric and cut it out.
2. Fold your fabric everywhere you see dashed lines on the template. Fold toward the wrong side of the fabric, and iron a sharp crease at every fold.
3. Fold the four flaps at the bottom of the box. Secure them with hot glue. Secure the sides at the flap with hot glue.

Finish

You can secure the lid of the box in several ways. Here are two of our favorites.

1. Glue a strip of ribbon to the bottom of the box and tie the loose ends over the top to hold the flap down.
2. Using glue, affix string, twine, or cord to the underside of the top flap. Sew (or glue) a button on the front of the box, about 1" below the top edge, and twirl the cord or string around the button to secure the flap.

POCKETED APRON

A daily apron is a wonderful thing to have, if it has pockets. Melody and I have several that serve as "work aprons," work meaning anything from cleaning house to cooking, sewing, crafting, running around, yelling at children, shushing the dog, late-night trysts (not really), or just picking up the living room. When I'm scuttling around trying to straighten a room and end up with hands full of Lego pieces, broken pencils, bits of chewed up dog toy, and misguided wine corks, I have a place in which they can rest until I find their proper homes—which is usually the junk drawer or the trash can, but at least I don't leave them under the sofa cushions.

An apron as gift wrap, you say? With multiple pockets, these hold great gifts that can then be folded up in the fabric and tied together in a bow with the sash. The theme of the gift can be cooking, gardening, art, children, whatever you need. But the lasting gift is that upon reuse, the apron can save the recipient a lot of backtracking and *where the hell is my phone?* (I spend at least 37 percent of the day, many days, just looking for my ringing phone.)

In an effort to really provide clear patterns for these projects, we enlisted the help of several sewists and crafters to do a test run for us. One of these tremendous helpers was Brittney Anderson, again. She said:

> *This was a really satisfying project—it took me maybe 15 minutes to complete with great results. The possibilities are really endless here, whether you fill the pockets with cleaning, crafty, or gardening supplies. It would make a great gift for a housewarming, birthday, father's day, hostess, on and on!*
>
> *The project could be adapted to just about any kind of person. I think it would be especially cute with a patchwork design or made of vintage linens. There's good space for appliquéing or embroidering a name or initials on a pocket. I also think this would be cute for kids to help around the house—load up the pockets with a sponge and wet wipes and let them scrub away. Another good idea would be one side made of an oilcloth material so you could get wet stuff (like said sponge) in there without making a mess! Seriously, this apron has so many options, I'm going to have to make one for every day of the week.*

Which is just what we wanted to hear, and even more! Take our ideas, her ideas, add your own. . . . This is one of our favorite projects. These aprons are a good use of smaller pieces left in your stash, and you can adjust the width of the apron to the recipient. Make a smaller version for a kid, one for a man in your life, or a wider version for ladies who actually weigh more than LeAnn Rimes. Geesh. Shouldn't we all?

Have

- Two pieces of fabric, 18" × 16"
- Iron
- Ribbon for the sash (At least 110" long to wrap around the back and tie in front; 70" or more to tie in back. Do the math according to your recipient.)
  NOTE: When you tie this apron into a cute little package, it will wrap up more sweetly with the longer ribbon.
- Straight pins

Optional, but Helpful

- Spray starch
- Rotary cutter and cutting mat

Prepare

1. Cut your two pieces of fabric according the dimensions specified.

2. Place the fabric right sides together. If the fabric is directional, stack the fabrics in the opposite directions (so the top of fabric A will be aligned with the bottom of fabric B).

3. Sew the pieces together with a ½" seam allowance, leaving at least a 6" opening.

4. Trim the corners, but be careful not to cut into your stitches (figure R1).

5. Turn the sewn piece inside out, poke out the corners with a chopstick or knitting needle if necessary, and iron it flat.

6. Iron the edges under at the 6" opening by ½" so they are even with the rest of the rectangle.

7. Stitch all the way across the side of the rectangle that has the opening, using a ⅛" seam allowance. While you only need to close up the opening, stitching all the way across the rectangle will give your project a more polished finish.

OPTIONAL

If you like, this is a nice place to use decorative stitches.

Make

1. Lay this stitched fabric flat, and fold the bottom edge up by 6", and this will form the pockets. (If your fabric was directional, make sure the pocket fabric isn't upside down.)

2. Stitch the sides all the way from the top to the bottom.
   OPTIONAL: Add a second row of stitches to reinforce the original seam.

3. Stitch the divisions in the pockets. You can make narrow pockets for pencils or paintbrushes, or wider pockets for notepads and cellphones. We stitched ours 5½" from each edge (figure R2).

Finish

You can use several options for the sash. We detail a few below. Remember to use a piece of ribbon at least 110" long, if you want to be able to wrap the ribbon around the back and tie it in front (as I do; it's so cute). Don't forget the longer ribbon will tie up into a prettier package in the end. Make sure to do the math based on your recipient—you don't want the straps to be too short! Keep in mind that some people wear these aprons at the hips; therefore, for a person with 36" hips, the ribbon would need to be around 108" to wrap all the way around and tie in a pretty bow in the front.

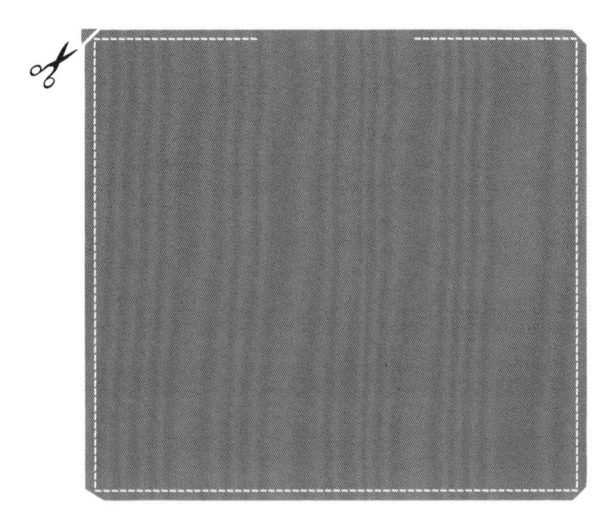

FIG. R1

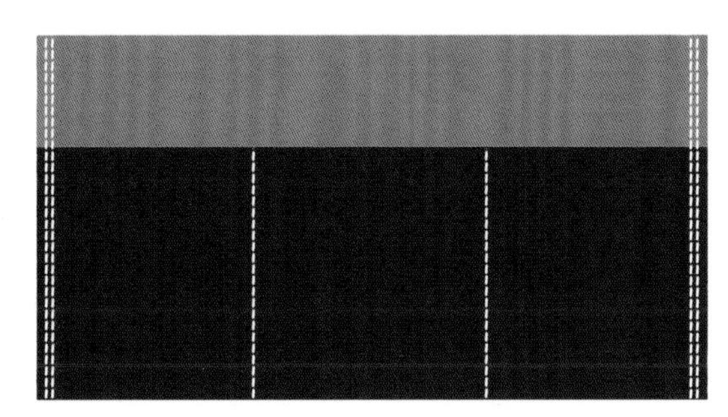

FIG. R2

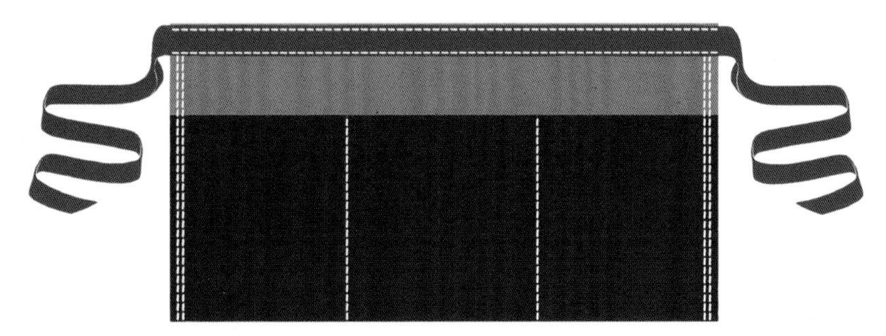

FIG. R3

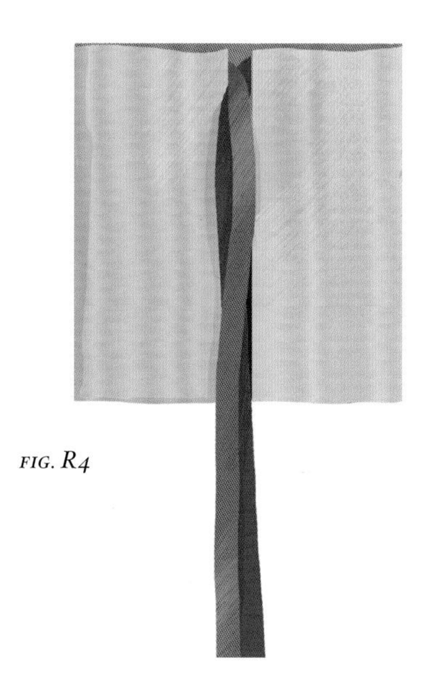

FIG. R4

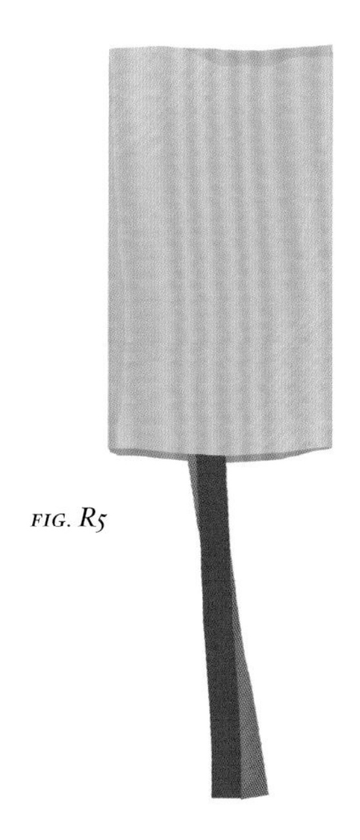

FIG. R5

OPTION 1

The easiest thing to do for the sash is to use a piece of ribbon ¾" or wider, and then determine the length based on the info above. Line up the center portion of the ribbon with the top edge of the apron. Top stitch the top and bottom edges of the ribbon to the apron (figure R3). Voilà!

OPTION 2

If you're using a piece of ribbon 1½" or wider, you can fold it over the top edge of the apron and stitch along the bottom edge, being sure to capture both sides of the ribbon with your stitching.

OPTION 3

If you're feeling fancy (like we were), sew a lovely, wide sash by cutting two strips of fabric approximately 3½" × 110" or longer.

TIP: Connect several shorter pieces to make the full length.

1. Sew the two pieces of fabric, right sides together, along both long edges and one of the short edges with a ¼" seam allowance.

2. Flip the sash inside out, and iron it flat. Tuck in the open end, and top stitch it all the way around the sash, as close to the edge as possible. Fold the sash in half across the top of your apron. Stitch along the bottom edge. The sash will appear narrow across the apron top but will be pretty and wide where it ties. Just like Alice in Wonderland.

FIG. R6

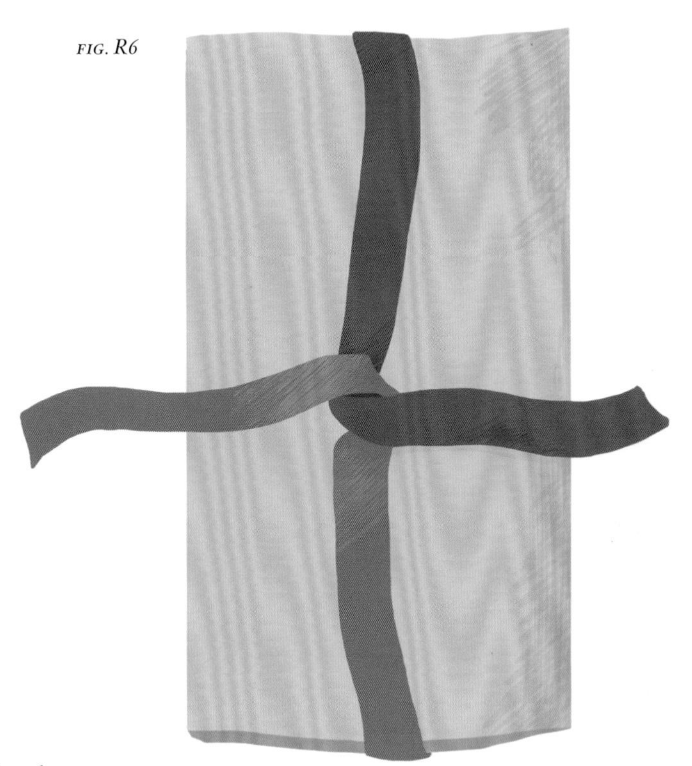

How to Wrap It All Up

Insert your gifts into the pockets and fold the left and right edge of the apron in so they meet in the middle. Run the ribbons downward (figure R4). Fold the apron in half, like a book. Adjust the ribbons so they are coming from the middle of the rectangle (figure R5). Run the ribbons in opposite directions around the long side of the rectangle, and have them meet in the center on the back side. Cross them over each other, and run them around horizontally to meet in the middle again on the other side (figure R6).

If one ribbon is distinctly longer than the other, run it around one more time to meet back at the same spot. And one more time, a beautiful bow!

THE ONLY GIFT IS A PORTION OF THYSELF.
RALPH WALDO EMERSON

Venir
bonbo
La saison
merveilleuse

LITTLE SNACK SACK

This project is a craft quickie. And there's no need to lock the door or straighten your frock afterward. Any little gift can be dropped right in, and then this project can be reused as a snack sack! A snack sack with style that no one will want to throw away! And the best thing is you can get three of these gems from one fat quarter of fabric.

HAVE

- Scrap fabrics, or one fat quarter
- Straight pins

OPTIONAL

- Button
- Velcro, if you don't like sewing buttons
- Trim

PREPARE

Cut your fabric to 7" × 18". (Our advice? Make lots at once!) To prevent the fabric from fraying, serge or zigzag stitch the edges, or just cut them with pinking shears.

MAKE

1. Lay the fabric out vertically, right side down.
2. Fold the top and bottom edges over toward the wrong side by ½".
3. Stitch these two folds with a ¼" seam allowance. Decorative stitches work nicely here.
4. Taking one of the ends that you just stitched, fold the fabric over toward the right side by 2½". Iron a sharp crease.

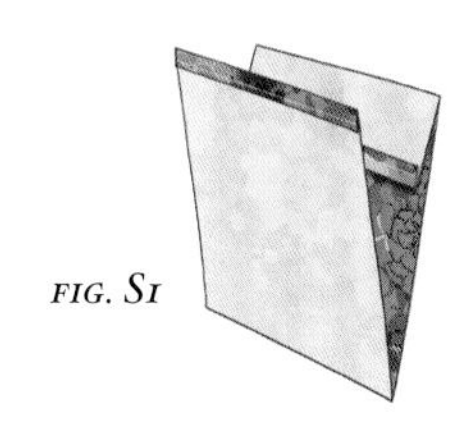

FIG. S1

5. Fold your newly creased edge over to the hemmed edge of the opposite end, right sides together. Allow the hemmed edge to be just a tiny bit lower than the folded edge (figure S1).
6. Stitch the left and right sides, with a ¼" seam allowance, leaving an opening at the top, where the folded edges are. As with any openings that you want to not fall apart, reinforce the stitching at top openings.

FINISH

Ready? Flip it right side out, and if necessary, poke out the corners with a knitting needle, or a chopstick.

TRY

- Here's where you can decide if you want to add trim to the front flap, or a pretty button and buttonhole.
- You can affix Velcro for a tighter closure, or just allow the opening to fold over, like those old sandwich bags that were always in a wad. But these won't wad like that. These are better.

5-MINUTE PARTY POUCHES

These Party Pouches are easier, cheaper, cuter, and more original than anything you'll find in the gift bag aisle at a big box store. Plus, they are a piece of cake to make. Make many of them at a time.

Have

- Paper for making a pattern
- Fabric scraps larger than your paper pattern by ½" on all sides
- Pinking shears
- Chopstick or knitting needle
- Twine or ribbon
- Straight pins

Optional

- Felt
- Buttons
- Hot Glue

Prepare

1. Cut out a rectangle of paper approximately the size you want your party pouches to be.
2. Sort out fabric scraps that are at least ½" larger than your template on all sides.
3. Stack two scraps right sides together, and trace your rectangular pouch pattern onto the top of the stack.

Make

1. Sew around three sides of the rectangle on your pencil lines, reinforcing your stitching several times at the beginning and end (the fourth side should be the opening of your pouch).
2. Using pinking shears, trim your fabric around the sewn edge and across the top pencil line, being careful to avoid cutting into your stitches.
3. Flip the bag inside out. If necessary, poke out the corners with a chopstick or knitting needle.

Finish

1. Find a piece of twine or ribbon long enough to wrap around your pouch and tie in a bow.
2. On the back side of the pouch, tack the twine or ribbon down in the center (about 1" from the top edge of the pouch) with your sewing machine, a hand stitch, or a dab of hot glue.
3. Simply tie the twine or ribbon around the top of the bag to close it. *So* pretty.

Try

- Sew a button to the front of the bag. Tie one end of your twine or string securely around the button, wrap it around the bag, and twist it around the button for closure.
- Make your bag out of felt, and cut a decorative edge across the top.

1878
PINAR
DEL RIO
SELECCIÓN

But Wait! There's More!

We also really like using interesting little containers for organization. Save Altoid tins for straight pins, cigar boxes for spools of thread, or other containers for *anything* that needs a cool box. Sometimes, pretty bits of jewelry come from etsy shops in clear-topped metal tins; I've even washed out one that held moisture balm (Melody gave me a great one from Sweet Petula). I put medicines in one for my bag, or keep the bracelets I'm into wearing this week in another on my vanity. The painted jars, bottles, or tins are beautiful storage vessels, or save a mixed nuts can and cover it with fabric or paper. Stash your stuff! ♛

BLACKBOARD WORK
BINNEY & SMITH CO.
NEW YORK
IODISED THROAT TABLETS
MEGGESON
DYSPEPSIA TABLETS
STOMACH COMFORT
MADE BY MEGGESON & CO. LTD., LONDON, ENGLAND
17 PIECES
NO. 922-DUMP-TRUCK
BABE RUTH
King of Swat
IN
PERFECT CONTROL
CASTLE FILMS
8mm OR 16mm
BERNZ-O-MATIC
Indelible
TYPE KIT
FOR
Cloth Marking
LOUIS MELIND COMPANY
CHICAGO
METAL BRIGHT
embossed gummed stars
10c
Sport Parade
CASTLE FILMS

7

FOR THE RIGID (GIFT, NOT PERSON), RECTANGULAR, OR BOOKISH

As a dying breed of people, we still love to play good board games. The Millers gave our kids something called Settlers of Catan last year, and much to my surprise, it rivals the computer. OK, it rivals the computer when we ban the computer, but still. They really do like this game. And there are several others in our house that still get playtime.

Games, books, framed art—these are the projects with which to wrap them. When you find a set of awesome '90s Neopets trading cards, a mid-century army serving tray, or an ancient copy of the Kama Sutra, this is your chapter. If you want to give fine art by your child, Twister, or the entire Harry Potter series, look to these ideas for wrapping your gift. I'd love a first edition of *Wuthering Heights*. If you find one, you'll send it, right? These projects will give your gift extra oomph. They are also great for giving Kindles, Nooks, iPads, iPods, iPhones, iAnything, or any other smart accessory. If your child is getting a laptop for graduation or a new school year, look here. (But don't tell my children, they'll be too jealous to live.)

As in most of our projects, we're trying to use the stuff lying about, cluttering up the joint, or the things we've had for so long and keep looking at thinking, "What will I ever use this for?" For the tote, check the back of your closet or the bottom of the old ironing pile to find a vintage concert T-shirt or a no-longer-worn button down.

Red Velvet
Vintage + Pretty things

BUTTON-DOWN SHIRT BAG

This bag is a really fun way to repurpose an old shirt. Melody sneakily used one from Greg's closet for our prototype, because the ones he no longer wears just weren't as cool as this one. *Shhhhhh.* The Button-Down Shirt Bag can carry along anything you need to carry. A bottle of wine, a few library books, or quick diaper bag needs. When Melody and I visit each other's homes, we're always bringing some food to share (we have six children between us, it's only fair), and we always need bags to hold the stuff.

Have

- Button-down shirt ready for a new life
- Sheerweight fusible interfacing (like Pellon 906F)
- Extra fabric for the lining of the bag
- Iron
- Spray starch
- Straight pins

Optional, but Helpful

- Quilter's clear grid ruler
- Metal straight edge
- Rotary cutter

Prepare

1. Iron the shirt. (You don't really need to iron the collar and sleeves, just the front and back.)

2. Stitch up the placket of the shirt so it can no longer open when it's unbuttoned.

3. If the shirt is lightweight, iron fusible sheerweight interfacing to the wrong sides of the front and the back of the shirt. This interfacing will keep the fabric from shifting or stretching while you are trying to cut and sew it.

4. Arrange the shirt so it is lying flat, with as few wrinkles as possible.

5. Cut a rectangle, measuring 1" wider and 2" taller than you want the final bag to be, through both layers of the center portion of the shirt (figure U1).
   TIP: We recommend using a quilter's clear grid ruler and rotary cutter here to keep the fabric flat and the angles at ninety degrees. Also, if the back of the shirt has any features like one of those funny loops or a pleat, you may need to cut the two sides separately to avoid an awkward placement of said features.

6. Cut two more pieces of fabric the same size as these rectangles for the bag lining. The easiest way to do this is to stack two layers of lining fabric with one of the shirt rectangles on top. Use the clear grid ruler and rotary cutter to cut along the edges of your shirt fabric.

7. On each of the four pieces of fabric, fold the top edge down toward the wrong side by ½" and then fold it a second time by 1". Sew across that edge with a ¾" seam allowance.
   TIP: We used a metal straight edge and a liberal amount of spray starch to fold the fabric perfectly straight across. Spray the top edge of the fabric with

starch and fold the fabric evenly over the straight edge. Touch the hot iron all the way across the fold to make a crease. Remove the straight edge, and iron the crease until the starch is dry. Repeat (without starch) for the 1" fold.

8. If the fabric rectangles have gotten a little off kilter during this process, just stack all four pieces with the newly hemmed edges aligned. Trim the sides and bottom with a rotary cutter and clear grid ruler to square up the edges.

Make

THE BAG

1. Put the shirt pieces right sides together. Pin along the side and bottom edges. Stitch those edges with a ½" seam allowance.

2. Do the same for the lining pieces.

3. Iron all the seams open.

THE STRAPS

1. There are several options for straps. You can use the technique for the Farmer's Daughter's Ribbon (see page 153) to make straps out of extra fabric from the shirt or any other scrap fabric. (If your fabric is lightweight, you may want to iron your fusible interfacing to the wrong side first.)

   TIP: You could be creative and use two men's neckties as the straps. Wide, sturdy ribbon or premade webbing would also work nicely.

   Because we were feeling fancy and, frankly, getting bored with ourselves one afternoon, we made our own wide silk straps. Well, Melody did. I watched and took notes. We know our roles and are very comfortable with them. Anyway, if you want to do the same, cut out two strips of silk (or whatever fabric you choose) 30" × 6". Take one strip, fold it lengthwise, right sides together, and pin it along the edge to create a piece that is 3" × 30". Repeat this process with the other strip.

2. On each strap, sew the pinned 30" edge with a ¼" seam allowance (leaving the short ends open).

3. Flip the fabric right side out (a chopstick or knitting needle is very handy to push the fabric through), and iron it flat. Top stitch over the two long edges with a ⅛" seam allowance.

4. Pin the ends of the straps to the wrong side of the bag lining. Once you have the straps pinned in place and have made sure they are even, sew the ends down as shown (figure U2). Trim off any excess fabric.

Finish

1. Drop the bag lining into the bag, wrong sides together, so that all the rough edges are hidden. Pin the top edges of the bag and the lining together, making sure the side seams are aligned.

2. Beginning somewhere near the center of your bag (away from the side seams), sew along the top edge with a ⅛" seam allowance.

3. Sew about halfway around the bag. Before you stitch over the final side seam, make sure the the bag lining is perfectly fitted to the bag. Sometimes, in spite of our best efforts, the top edge of one of the bags is larger than the other. If that is the case, sew a new side seam on the bigger of the two with a larger seam allowance (only at the top; after a few inches, the new seam can run back into the old one). Typically, this small adjustment won't be visible in the finished piece (figure U3).

4. Finish stitching the top edge of the bag.

FIG. U1

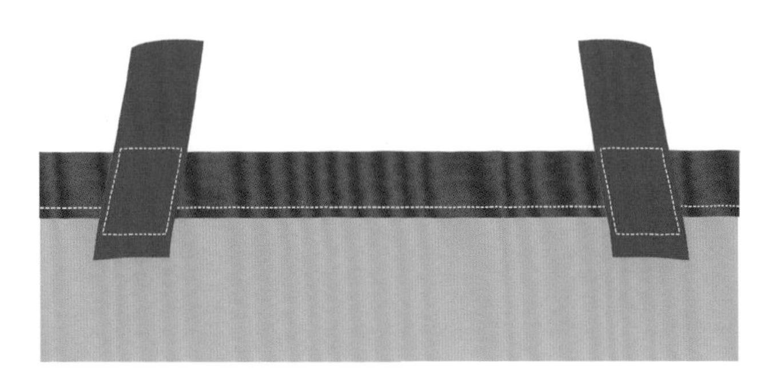

FIG. U2

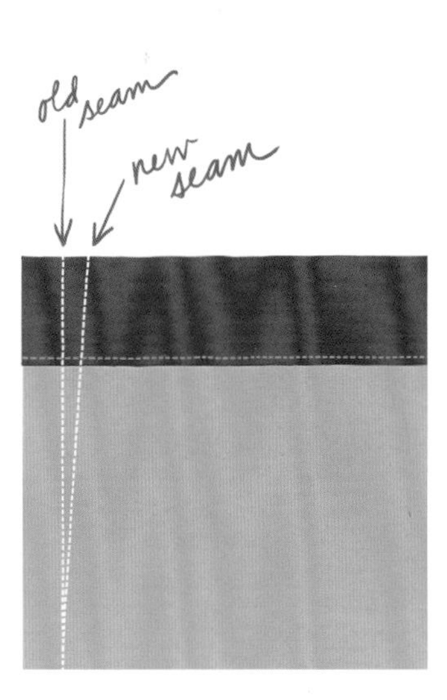

FIG. U3

WE DON'T STOP PLAYING BECAUSE WE GROW OLD;
WE GROW OLD BECAUSE WE STOP PLAYING.
✿ GEORGE BERNARD SHAW ✿

CASTLE

PILLOWCASE POUCH

This is one of our favorite projects, not only because it's quick and simple, but because it is so versatile, too. It's one of the first reusable gift wrap projects Melody ever came up with, long before there was an idea for a book. If you're giving something rectangular and flat, like a book, a framed photo, or a game, here is one of the simplest and loveliest ways in which to give it. And it's one of the best things to keep on hand for regiving as well.

Have

- Coordinating fabrics for the front and back of the pouch
- Trim, rickrack, or buttons, if you like

Prepare

Decide how large you want your pouch to be. If, for instance, you're giving a book, you might want the pouch to be several inches taller than the book, and at least twice as wide, in order for the fabric to wrap around. There is plenty of flexibility here. You can also piece several fabrics together to make up one of the sides, or appliqué letters, numbers, or shapes onto your fabric. Or, sew a pocket onto one of the sides to insert a card or note.

Make

1. Cut both fabrics to the desired width + 2" and the desired height + 1". You may want to cut the fabric with pinking shears, or serge or zigzag stitch the edges to prevent fraying.
2. For each fabric, on the end of the rectangle where the pouch will open, fold and iron the fabric toward the wrong side by ½". Then, fold by 1" and iron again. Sew across each fabric with a ¾" seam allowance.
   OPTIONAL: Add trim to one or both of these edges.
3. Place the two rectangles right sides together, with the top edges aligned. Sew the sides and bottom with a ½" seam allowance, reinforcing the seam at the top.
4. Trim the bottom two corners. Flip the pouch right side out.

Finish

Insert your gift, and fold the excess fabric around. Finish by wrapping the package with ribbon or twine or one of our garland accessories. Or, make one of our other accessories, like the ravishing Resplendent Rose (page 163), and pin it in place.

VARIATION

In the early part of 2011, we decided to make a really cool newsprint promo piece. Then, we came up with a fabric pouch in which to mail it to very special recipients. (Like, the kind that might want us to design stuff and make us rich, right?) This fabric mailer is much like the pillowcase pouch, except a little more polished. The entire thing folds perfectly in half and buttons in place. And it is also perfect for giving flat rectangular gifts like books or picture frames. Here's how you can make one.

Have

- Three coordinating fabrics
- Rickrack or trim
- Button(s) for the closure
- Straight pins

Prepare

1. Decide how large you want your finished pouch to be when it is unfolded (remembering that your gift will reside in one half of it, and the other half will fold on top). Make note of the finished width and height (figure V1).
   - Fabric A will back of the pouch, and the part you see when it is folded.
   - Fabric B will be the other side of the pouch, which will be hidden when folded.
   - Fabric C will be a lining that you will see at the opening of the pouch.

2. Cut fabric A to your finished width + 1" and height + 1".

3. Cut fabric B to your finished width - 2" and height + 1".

4. Cut fabric C to 6" wide and the height + 1".
   NOTE: Cut with pinking shears, or serge or zigzag stitch the edges to prevent fraying.

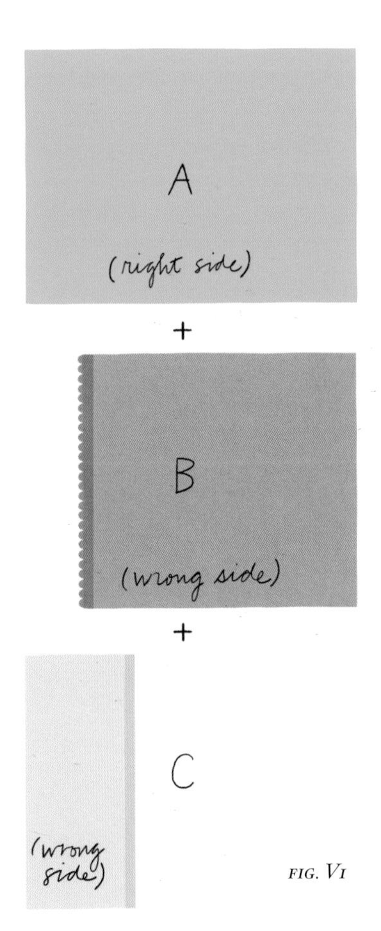

FIG. V1

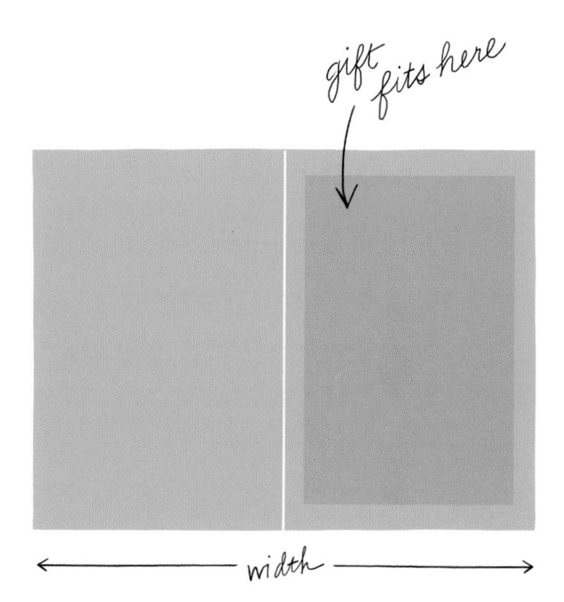

FIG. V2

Make

1. On fabric B, fold and iron the left edge (the edge of the opening of the pouch) toward the wrong side by ½", twice. Pin a piece of trim across this edge, and sew it with a ¼" seam allowance (or the necessary allowance to attach your trim).

2. On fabric C, fold and iron the right edge under by ½". Sew with a ¼" seam allowance.

3. Stack the fabrics as follows:
   - Fabric A is on the bottom right side up.
   - Fabric B is right side down on top of fabric A, with the top, bottom, and right edges aligned.
   - Fabric C is right side down on top, with the left (unhemmed) edge aligned with fabric A (figure V2).

4. Pin these three fabrics in place, and sew around all four edges with a ½" seam allowance. Trim the corners, and flip all sections right side out.

Finish

Fold your finished pouch in half and mark where you want your button(s) to go. Sew and cut buttonholes slightly wider than your button(s). With the pouch neatly folded, use a pencil to mark directly through the center of your buttonhole so you know where to sew your button.

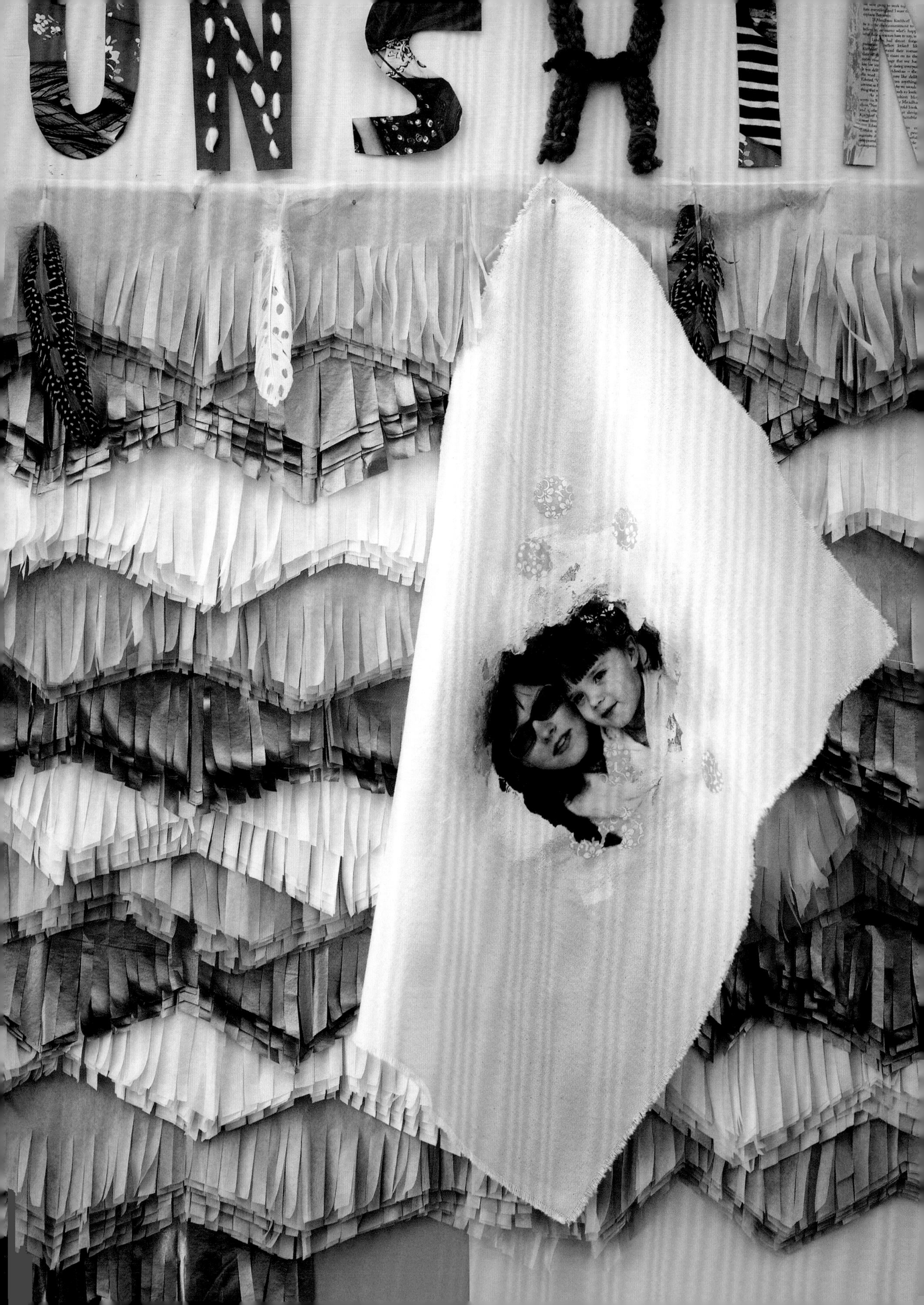

J'S IMAGE TRANSFER CANVAS

When we exhibited at Surtex in the Spring of 2011 (an international trade show for surface and print design that convenes in New York each May), we met the loveliest new friend, Jaimie Harris from *This is J*. Our particular corner of the show was pretty quiet most days, so we had lots of time to learn about Jaimie and her business, and to tell her about the exciting things we were up to, like writing this book. Apparently, Jaimie is an old hand at reusable gift wrap, and she shared some of her favorite ideas with us. As she began to describe the technique used for this project, transferring a photocopied image to canvas, Melody realized that she used to do that exact same technique in her paintings. The coincidence was perfect, and we decided this project must be included in our book. Jaimie was thrilled! She'll be famous, and it will be all because of this book!

Our favorite thing about this project is that the gift wrap is an actual piece of art. Don't think you're an artist? Wait 'til you try this project—you'll be famous among your friends and family for your crazy skills.

Have

- Canvas (We used undyed painter's canvas, but any cotton canvas should do.)
- Photocopied or laser-printed images, or images cut from magazines (Note: Ink jet prints will not work here, but vintage catalogues will!)
- Clear acrylic medium (You can use glossy or matte; we prefer the gel, not the liquid.)
- Paintbrush
- Palette knife
- Paper towels

Optional

- Other colors of acrylic paint (especially white)
- Few decorative papers to add in

Prepare

1. Cut out some images from magazines or find some lovely pictures to photocopy. Family photos, especially old ones, are favorites here. Copy the image using a standard black-and-white photocopier or a laser printer (in which case color prints will work as well, but we stand by the black-and-white variety). We like to make a few different sizes of the same image so we have options later on. Also, remember that any text in your image will be reversed in the final piece.

2. Iron the canvas. Cut the canvas large enough to wrap around your gift.

3. Wrap the canvas around your gift. We typically just fold it over the sides and back as neatly as possible. On the front side of the gift, make some light pencil marks on the canvas to show where the image should go. Unwrap the gift, and put it aside.

4. Brush a coat of acrylic medium on the canvas in the general area where the image will go. Make sure the canvas is saturated.

5. If you want, brush in some white acrylic paint, just a little here and there—and possibly even a light color or two. A fleck of yellow, a spot of turquoise. . . . These will peek through your image and add a nice texture to the finished piece. (And, hey, when you're finished with that paintbrush, put it in some water. Once the paint dries, your brush is a goner.) You can also add some little paper bits here and there. Just be sure to coat the top of them with acrylic medium after you stick them down.

Make

1. Roughly cut out your photocopied image. Extra white space around the image is fine. Use a palette knife (the cheap plastic variety works great here) to spread a generous layer of acrylic medium over the image itself; stick to covering the printed bits, not the surrounding paper. Then spread a layer of medium over the canvas where the image will go (acrylic dries quickly, so the first coat on your canvas should be pretty dry by now). Stick the paper *face down* on the canvas, lightly smoothing out any air bubbles with your fingers.

2. Allow the acrylic medium to dry thoroughly. This may take several hours, but you shouldn't have to wait overnight.

3. Once the medium is completely dry, bring a few paper towels and a bowl of water to your work area. You are going to remove the paper from the canvas, leaving the image embedded in the dried acrylic medium. Fold and wet a paper towel. Use it to brush over your paper so that it is saturated with water.

4. Begin lightly wiping the paper. The first coat of paper should come off pretty easily; you can almost peel it off with your fingers. A thin, fuzzy layer of paper that is a little harder to remove will be left behind. (Being a bit craft-challenged, I thought this sounded difficult. It is *not*.)

5. Using the paper towel, gently scrub the image with small circular motions. Your goal is to get all the paper fuzz off, while not removing the ink of the image itself. You will find that while the image is wet, it may appear that all the paper is gone. However, the image might have a cloudy appearance when it dries, which means the lightest layer of paper fuzz is still left. When you get to this layer, you can actually rub away the fuzz with wet fingertips. Just keep burnishing the image until all the fuzz is gone.

Finish

1. Melody particularly loves the rough edges of the image, and the way that some bits of it come off during the paper-removal process. However, she gets really happy after adding just a few final touches. Sometimes she'll paint a little black over some of the rougher spots of the image. Then, she'll use white or even a little color to brush around the image, overlapping some of the edges. She's even used sandpaper to roughen up the edges a little more. Now is a time to have fun. Use your fingertips and smear some paint around a little. Add a few flecks of color. Is there a spot you don't like? Cover it with a pretty shape of paper, and brush over with your acrylic medium. Or, do a quick burst of spray paint to add a little color around your image (Mel has a thing for fluorescent pink).

2. Admire your artwork! When it's dry, wrap it back around your gift and secure it with some ribbon, cord, or twine.

But Wait! There's More!

If you've time for nothing else, these sorts of gifts are also great to wrap with a piece of fabric, or a scarf, in the Japanese tradition of *tsutsumi*. Our friend Jaimie suggested keeping on hand a few of those Pashmina scarves that can be purchased very cheaply in certain areas of different cities, like Chinatown in New York. When she finds a good price, she buys several. (We've been lucky to find vintage Vera scarves and the like at our local thrift stores.) Compared to what you'll be picking up at big box stores—the gift bag, tissue, a bow or curly ribbon, and a card—you'll end up with something that is not only less expensive but also totally reusable.

If you wrap up the gift in a scarf, your recipient can wear the wrapping! We did this exact thing when purchasing a birthday gift for my daughter's friend recently. She wanted to give a bracelet and ring that we had just purchased, and we were meeting the friend for lunch right away. After realizing we had no gift bag (I know, bad example I am), we glanced around the store and spied a beautiful lightweight scarf, half off at $5.00. Voilà! Wrap the ring, cinch the scarf with the bracelet, and it was truly a gift, in a gift, sealed with a gift! ♛

8

THE EXTRAS

There is most certainly some truth to the notion that if you are going to do something, you might as well do it all the way—or put alternately, do it right. I admit, I struggle with this. Often I've started a project, such as sewing a little pair of pants for our youngest, and wound up wanting to just staple it all together to *get it done.* But Melody will not accept this, so she will finish it for me. Her penchant for finishing things right is why I try very hard to save my projects for when she's around. I'm smart like that.

This chapter is where you have the opportunity to ice the cake. Take your *pulchritudinous* package (a ten-cent word, *thankyouverymuch,* meaning "lovely, beautiful, or agreeable," as I was getting really bored with those adjectives so I sought out my thesaurus), and dress it up in all its glory. Add these accessories to any of our gift packaging projects. Make them in advance, stash them away, and when you need to wrap something in a hurry, you'll be able to whip up a gorgeous package in no time.

The ideas here make great use of the bits of leftover trim, lonely buttons, the last few inches of a great ribbon, a bandanna, even old linens or T-shirts. Scrap fabrics get freed from their plastic storage tubs, drawers get cleaned out, and it is all turned into pretties. Win/Win.

Reuse these projects by pinning the flowers into hair or on a headband. Clip bows on a bag or even a belt. Attach them to a small magnet, and they are beautiful on a bulletin board or as interesting art hangers on your fridge. Obviously, any extras you have can also be saved for other packages.

When we were trying these projects on for size in our own homes, Melody strung the gift garland from painted bottle to painted jar to painted bottle, which made a great mantle top piece! Ribbons can be used in clothing, on handmade bags, in hair, around other gifts. Wrap one around an old jar to create a container for your desk, workroom, vanity, the pantry—anywhere you need some organization with chutzpah. A grouping of paper or fabric flowers glued onto gardener's wire would make a sweet bouquet that will never die. Put it in a painted bottle!

FARMER'S DAUGHTER'S RIBBON

This project is essentially like making a quilt binding. When Melody first learned to make binding, she realized along the way that it would make a very sweet ribbon, especially when composed of lots of little scraps. The process is not difficult at all, especially for you quilters. Maybe you'll find yourself stuck in the house under a pile of snow, or under a pile of sick children, and the time will be just right to whip up some ribbon. The ribbon here is 1" wide, but feel free to adjust the width accordingly. Here's the math: (desired width × 2) + 1".

Have

- Assortment of fabric scraps
- Cutting mat
- Rotary cutter
- Scissors

Prepare

Cut your scraps into 3" wide strips, any length.

Make

1. Trim the ends to make them square.
2. Place the first two strips right sides together, with one short end aligned.
3. Stitch that end with a ¼" seam allowance. Continue adding strips in this manner until you have reached your desired length. (We like to make lots, and keep it on hand for last-minute wrapping.)
4. Press open the seams.
5. Lay your ribbon horizontally, right side down on the ironing board. Mist it with spray starch. Fold the bottom edge up by ½", and iron, making a sharp crease. Then fold the top edge down by ½", and iron. Press well. Make that iron work it.
6. Fold the pressed edges together, right sides out, edges aligned carefully, and iron everything in place.

Finish

1. With your machine, stitch a ⅛" seam allowance on the left and right edges.
2. Roll the ribbon and store it.
3. Remember where you put it.

Try

Another creative way to do this is to sew up a patchwork of scrap fabrics, then cut the entire patchwork into 3" strips. Sew the 3" strips end-to-end, and proceed with instructions 4 through 6.

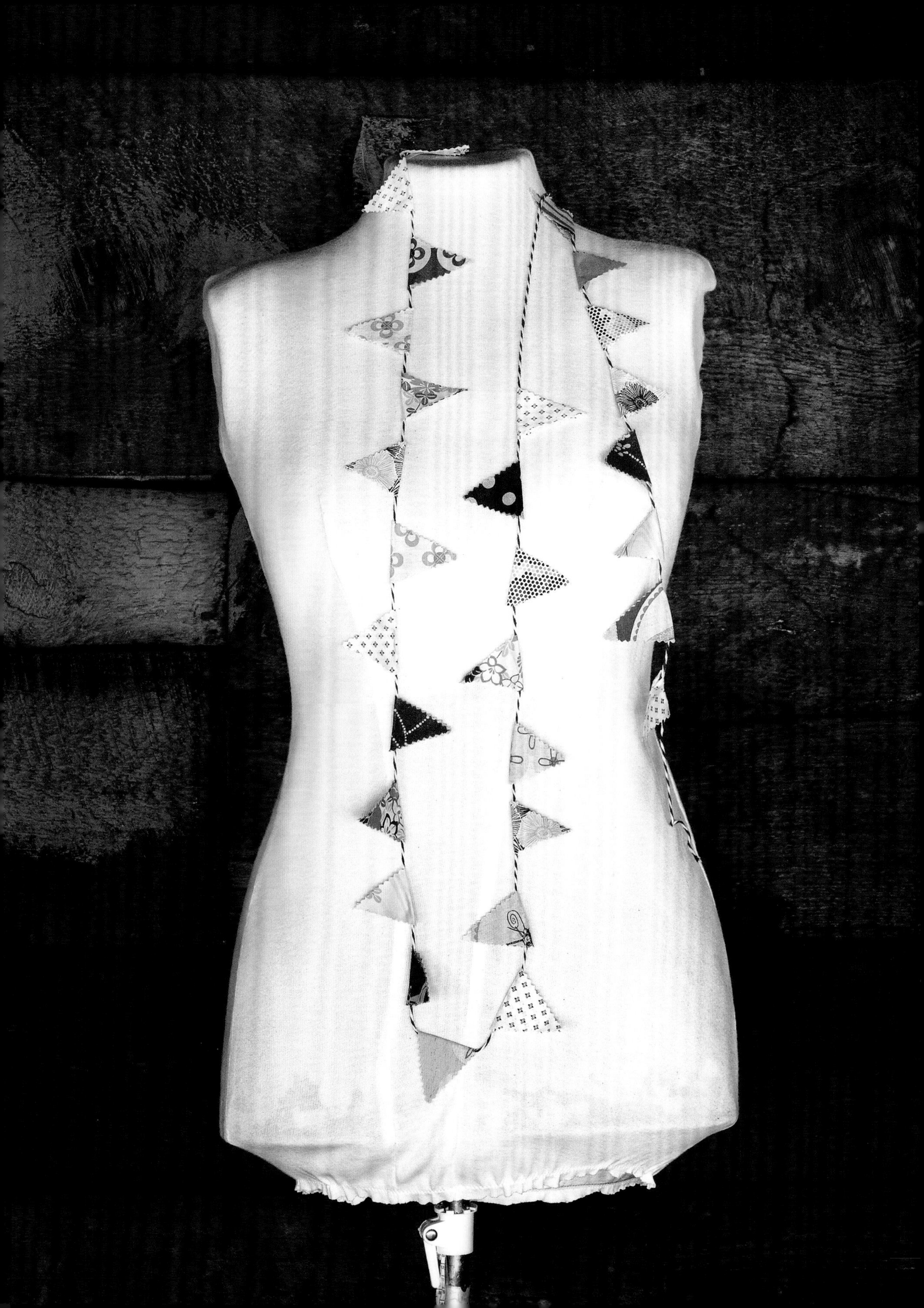

FESTIVE FLAG GARLAND

Taking the idea that flag garlands cheer up any space (think: kid's rooms, birthday parties, storefronts), we decided that a miniature version would be a delightful addition to a gift. Melody keeps one strung in her dining room right now, just because it makes her smile. She's just simple that way.

HAVE

- Assortment of scraps
- String, cord, thin ribbon, twine, or any item with which you'd like to string your garland
- Pinking shears
- Fabric glue, or fusible web (Stitch Witchery works great here.)
- Straight pins

PREPARE

1. Determine the size of your garland triangles. Ours are about 1½" wide at the widest point, and 2" high. Yours can be any size you like.

2. Iron all your scraps flat. Each scrap needs to be wider than your intended triangle and at least twice the height.

3. Fold the scraps in half, wrong sides together, and iron a quick crease.

4. Using pinking shears, cut out the two long sides of your triangle so that the horizontal top side of the triangle is on the fold of your fabric (figure Y1).

MAKE

Time to string the triangles! Fold each triangle over the twine, cord, or whatever you choose, and secure them with fabric glue or fusible web.

TIP: We tore off short lengths of Stitch Witchery and ironed them to the inside of the unfolded triangles, using parchment paper to prevent sticking. When it was time to put the triangles on the twine, we simply folded them over and quickly touched them with the iron to adhere the front to the back. The Stitch Witchery adhered to the twine as well as the fabric, keeping the triangles from slipping.

FINISH

Continue to attach all the flag pieces until you reach the length of garland you planned. Sha-zaaam! A lovely, reusable wrapping accessory! It's a necklace, a mantle decoration, hair ribbon, or um, a stylish "leash" for your crazy toddler while in the mall! Personally, I don't recommend malls, but a leash? Could be extremely helpful.

FIG. Y1

NEWSPAPER FLOWER

It's possible that the Millers are one of the last few families on the planet still subscribing to the Sunday *Times* (what with the Internet, and all). They just love getting that huge bulk of newspaper every weekend and knowing there are hours worth of interesting stories inside. However, by the end of the week, there's, you know, all that newspaper lying around. One day, Melody just decided to make something with it, and well, she wanted that something to be pretty. Here's her creation. And the rest of the newspaper? It's in Greg's beloved composter. Really. It was his favorite birthday gift ever.

Have

- Some newspaper or other lightweight paper, like magazine pages or tissue paper
- Sharp scissors
- Ornament for the center of your flower, like a felt ball, a pompom, or a button
- Hot glue, stapler, or needle and thread
- Newspaper Flower template (page 183)

Optional

- Small circle of felt for the back of the flower
- Magnet, Velcro, or a hairpin for the back of the flower

Prepare

1. Cut out a rough square of newspaper, larger than 8" × 8". Cut through about eight sheets at once to get a quick stack (figure Z1).
2. Cut out the template.
3. Fold a stack of four sheets into quarters. Line your template up with the inside corner of your folded stack (so that the petals point out toward the loose edges of the paper). Trace and cut. Cut a notch between the petals where you see the dotted lines on the template as well.
4. Repeat with the other four sheets.

Make

1. Unfold, separate, and rotate the layers so that the petals are no longer perfectly aligned (figure Z2).
2. Staple once in the middle or stitch a few times with needle and thread. (Confession: Melody actually sticks the whole thing in her sewing machine and runs a few stitches through.)
3. Use hot glue to affix a button or pompom or felt ball to the center of the flower.
4. Fold the petals up from the center of the flower until it is nicely filled out. Wrap the petals around the object in the center to make them stand up. Make it messy, work it, that's it. . . . (figure Z3)

FIG. Z1

FIG. Z2

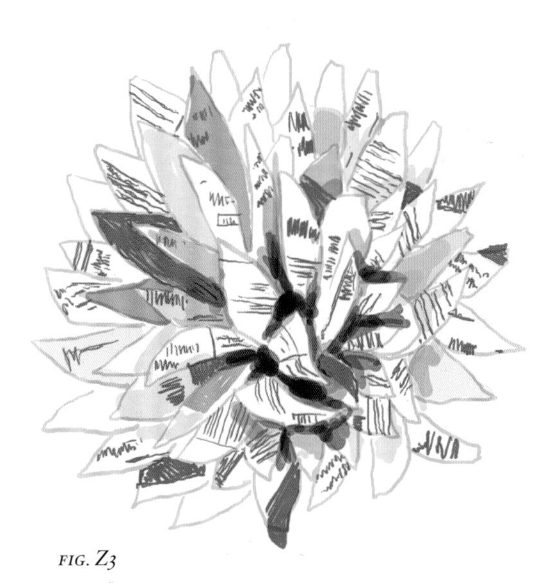

FIG. Z3

Try

- ☞ Glue a small circle of felt to the back of your flower. Affix a hairpin to the felt so the recipient can reuse it as a sweet hair accessory.
- ☞ Glue a magnet to the back of the flower so the recipient can keep it on her refrigerator.
- ☞ Stick a piece of Velcro to the back of the flower, and use its mate to attach it to your gift.

What? We need to give you more? You can't think for yourself?! Think, think! Oh, OK. Here's one more. . . .

- ☞ A variation of this would work great on fabric as well. We recommend heavily starching your fabric scraps and, one at a time, ironing them into crisp quarters. Then, cut the petals out according to the template. Unfold and stack four to six flowers, and use hot glue to stick one on top of the other, pinching in the middle to help the petals stand up. Finish by adding an ornament in the center. Like, a felt ball!

THE DIFFERENCE BETWEEN ORDINARY
AND EXTRAORDINARY IS THAT LITTLE EXTRA.

◇◇◇◇◇ ANONYMOUS ◇◇◇◇◇

RESPLENDENT ROSE

Try this simple and easy way to make a fabric flower. There are two variations: one producing a smaller bud and the other a fuller bloom. If you've never used elastic thread before, let this flower be your introduction, and you'll be hooked. This stretchy stuff is surprisingly easy to work with and very versatile. If you want an even smaller bud than the two flowers we're describing, cut your fabric at 24" wide and 2" high.

Have

- Elastic thread
- Assortment of scrap fabrics that are pretty together
- Iron
- Scissors
- Needle and thread

Optional, but Helpful

- Rotary cutter and cutting mat
- Quilter's grid ruler
- Felt or pretty scrap fabrics for leaves
- Hot glue

Prepare

1. Cut your scraps on the bias into 3" strips. Cutting on the bias will prevent the edges of the flower from fraying.
   TIP: Scraps not quite big enough to cut on the bias? Sew a bunch of them together, patchwork style, iron the seams open, and then cut the entire finished block on the bias into long strips
2. Sew the strips end-to-end with a ¼" seam allowance until you have one strip 40"–60" long, depending on how full you want the flower to be.
3. Iron open the seams.
4. Wind some elastic thread into your bobbin. Do this by hand. Don't stretch it too tight as you're winding. Put the bobbin in your machine.
5. Put regular thread on your spool. Set your machine to the longest stitch, and set your tension to the highest number.

Make

1. Sew along the edge of your fabric using a ½" seam allowance. Be sure to reverse over your stitches at the beginning and end to keep the elastic from unraveling. Trim any excess thread.
2. Time to wind up the flower. Start at one end of the strip, with your fingers on the elastic side. Begin to

roll up the elastic edge of the strip. Keep the elastic side gathered firmly together, and keep the other side loose. Experiment to see how tightly you want to wind your flower.

3. Once it is all rolled up, looking like a *resplendent rose*, we've found the easiest way to hold it together is to pass a threaded needle back and forth through the elastic end of the flower several times, being sure to catch all of the layers. After five or six passes, tie off the thread and snip the ends.

4. If you're *really* detail oriented, use scissors to round off the corner where the strip ends on the outside of your rose—just looks more petal-like that way.

Finish

1. One of our favorite ways to polish off this flower is by adding leaves. If you have felt, cut two big leaves, one larger than the other. Hot glue the entire base of the bud onto the end of a leaf, then attach the other leaf in such a way that you think it looks right (or covers up any messy spots).

2. If you do not have felt, stack two pieces of scrap fabric wrong sides together and lightly draw a big leaf shape on top. Go over your entire outline with the applique stitch on your sewing machine. Trim along the outside of your stitch, being careful not to cut into the stitching itself. No chopsticks or knitting needles are required to turn it out the right way; it is perfect as it is.

   NOTE: Don't forget to take out the elastic thread and set your machine back to its regular settings, or you'll be terribly surprised the next time you sit down to sew!

VARIATION

This flower is very similar to the one you just made, except without the rough edges of the fabric. By using a wider strip of fabric and folding it in half, we are able to have an even more full and polished bloom.

Prepare

1. From your scraps, cut strips of fabric 6" wide. They do not have to be cut on the bias.

2. Sew the strips end-to-end with a ¼" seam allowance until you have a strip 40"–60" long, depending on how full you want the flower to be.

3. Iron open the seams.

4. Fold and iron the entire strip lengthwise, wrong sides together, so that it is now 3" wide.

5. Again, wind some elastic thread into your bobbin. You'll do this by hand. Don't stretch it too tight as you're winding. Put the bobbin in your machine.

6. Put regular thread on your spool. Set your machine to the longest stitch, and set your tension to the highest number.

Make

1. Sew through both layers of the edge of your fabric (the rough edge, not the folded one), using a ½" seam allowance. Be sure to reverse over your stitches at the beginning and end to keep the elastic from unraveling. Trim any excess thread.

2. Wind up the flower just like before. Start at one end of the strip, with your fingers on the elastic side. Begin to roll up the elastic edge of the strip. Keep the elastic side gathered firmly together, and keep the other side loose. Experiment to see how tightly you want to wind your flower.

3. Once it is all rolled up, pass a threaded needle back and forth through the elastic end of the flower several times, being sure to catch all of the layers. After five or six passes, tie off the thread and snip the ends.

Finish

Again, add some leaves!

BOWTIE BOW

We've so loved seeing a resurgence in bowties. My teenaged son is even wearing one with short-sleeved button-down shirts when he goes out with his friends. But possibly, that's because he's just a nerd.

This little ditty was created by Melody after she made a patchwork quilt for Iliana, using 6" squares of fabric. She ended up with stacks of leftover squares and was always looking for different ways to use them. One day, she put a few together and realized, *hey! Great bows!*

This project is super quick, no sew, no glue, and all simple. A quilter might be thrilled to untie the bow and reuse the squares in a project. For others, it could be a hair bow to glue on a headband or attach to a long piece of ribbon. Glue a pin back to it, and it goes on a bag, a shirt, a belt, anything. Glue a magnet on the back, and it is an adorable be-bowed magnet. Glue it on the top of your favorite pen or pencil, and maybe you'll have better luck keeping up with your writing instrument than I do.

Have

- Four 6" squares of fabric (or a million, whichever)
- Pinking shears

Make

1. Trim the edges of your squares with pinking shears to keep them from fraying.
2. Take the three squares you want to use in the bow, and do approximately four accordion-style folds on each. Put them in a stack.
3. Take fourth square and fold it into a triangle. Roll the point of triangle back down toward the long folded side. (If you were anywhere between the ages of ten and thirty in the '80s, you'll know the bandanna we folded and put in our hair? Like that, basically.)
4. Take that folded fourth piece, and tie it one time around the center of the accordioned squares tightly.
5. Fluff out the folds into a bow. Melody may or may not spend more than an hour getting it "just right."

Try

If you don't want the rough edges of the fabric included in your bow, take two pieces of fabric, about 6" × 12", and sew them right sides together with a 1/4" seam allowance, leaving a 4" opening across the bottom edge of the rectangle. Turn the rectangle right side out, sew up the open end, fold it accordion style, and tie it in the center, like above.

VARIATIONS ON A FELT BALL THEME

We are absolutely in love with felt balls. If you don't share our affinity, this section may not be for you. But you're missing out. These projects are so simple, but they amp up the cute factor of your package by about a million. We particularly love that *no felt balls are harmed in the making of these projects,* so if your recipient wants to unstring them and use them for something else, she totally can.

Left intact, these little darlings accessorize anything from a ponytail to a handbag to the fridge door. They are adorable Christmas tree ornaments, and as I write this, I'm wearing a garland as a trés chic necklace. Wrap one several time around your wrist, and you're the most colorful bracelet wearer at the party. That's super important, right?

GARLAND

Have

- Again, a supply of felt balls
- Embroidery needle
- Embroidery or other heavy thread (We used metallic thread. Ooooooh, pretty.)

Make

Thread the needle, and poke through the center of the felt balls, either spacing them a certain number of inches apart or stringing them solidly. Repeat until you have the length you want. Easy-peasy.

ORNAMENT

Have

- And once again, a supply of felt balls, different sizes are fun
- The embroidery needle
- Lightweight jewelry wire

Make

1. String the balls onto the wire, using the needle if necessary. Our wire was particularly lightweight, so we did need the needle.

2. Once you have ten or more on the string, depending on how large you want the ornament to be, start wrapping the wire around itself, causing the balls to

gather in a bunch. Think grapes. They can be in a tight bunch, or loose and standing apart from each other.

3. Use the wire to continue wrapping into and around the balls, just until everything feels secure. Use the last bit of wire to wrap your creation directly onto your package, or apply a pin back or magnet—your call!

LOLLIPOP BOUQUETS

Have

- Surprise! A supply of felt balls, larger and smaller
- Jewelry wire that is a thick enough gauge to stand up on its own and push through a felt ball
- Wire clippers

Make

1. Snap the wire into 4" segments until you have ten or so pieces. Take each piece, and gently push it through a ball.

2. Hook the top ½" or so of wire back toward the ball, then push it back into the top of the ball to hold the ball firm. Hey! A sweet little lollipop! We found ten or eleven made a great bouquet, but do as many as you like.

3. Attach them to a bottle or jar with twine or hot glue them on a package, and as the other projects, these make great accessories on nearly anything after the original purpose of adorning your present is past.

READER'S DIGEST
Condensed
BOOKS
THE
READER'S DIGEST
ASSOCIATION
Summer 1954
Selections
READER'S DIGEST
Best loved
Books
FOR YOUNG
READERS
Wuthering
Heights
Summer 1953
Selections
Vol XIV
THE
READER'S DIGEST
ASSOCIATION
READER'S DIGEST
Condensed
BOOKS

PAPER PUNCH GARLAND

Adding a garland to a package is like putting on your favorite necklace after getting dressed. Sometimes, it is the final yum that really makes your package tasty. One of the simplest garlands is a string of paper cutouts; use a paper punch or just a good pair of scissors to add this *delicious* handmade treat.

Have

- Regular to heavyweight paper (Check your recycling bin!)
- String, cord, twine, or very thin ribbon
- Paper punch (that makes 1" shapes or larger) or a good pair of scissors
- Double-sided tape or craft glue

Make

1. If you have a paper punch: punch out enough shapes to extend the length of your string. If you don't have a paper punch: put two pieces of paper wrong sides together and cut out a simple shape like a star (or heart! or your favorite African nation! or whatever!). Repeat until you have enough pairs of shapes to attach to your string.

2. Use either double-sided tape or craft glue to stick two shapes wrong sides together with the string sandwiched in the middle.

3. Tah-dah! Even *more* garland!

Try

Stack your paper shapes with the wrong sides together and run them through your sewing machine, stitching a line straight down the center. Pull the same length of thread between each shape for a continuous garland.

TECHNIQUES AND TEMPLATES

To use these templates, photocopy them at the size indicated or download and print actual-size patterns from www.roostbooks.com/rubystarwrapping. Please use the templates from this book for your own personal use.

To use the templates for the Gift Card Elephant Softie and the Gift Card Truck Softie, photocopy the templates (enlarging them as indicated) or print the PDFs on 8 ½" × 11" paper. If printing from the PDF, tape the two sheets end-to-end *without* any overlap. There may be a slight gap in your elephant/truck shape where the printer didn't print all the way to the edge, but just pencil the lines back in to make the shape whole. The pattern extends to the edge of the page.

Ladder Stitch

When you need to sew up an opening on a stuffed project, the ladder stitch is perfect. Work carefully, and you won't even be able to see the stitch when you're finished!

1. Tuck the raw edges at your opening inside, and pinch the fabric shut. Make a nice crease with your fingers on both pieces of fabric.

2. Loop your thread through your needle as shown, and tie a nice big knot at the end (figure 1).

3. Pull your needle out from the inside of the seam, on the side of your opening where the fabric is stitched together. The knot should keep the thread from pulling all the way through (figure 2).

4. Your goal is to run the needle through in the following path, always putting the needle horizontally through the crease of the fabric (figure 3).

5. Starting at the top, run your needle in and back out (about ⅛") horizontally through the crease of the fabric. Pull the thread all the way through (figure 4).

6. Directly below the point where the needle exited the top piece of fabric, insert it into the crease of the piece below. Do the same horizontal stitch (figure 5).

7. Directly above where the needle just exited the bottom piece of fabric, insert it back into the top crease (figure 6).

8. Continue in this manner until you have the entire opening stitched up. Tie a small knot at the end, and snip your thread.

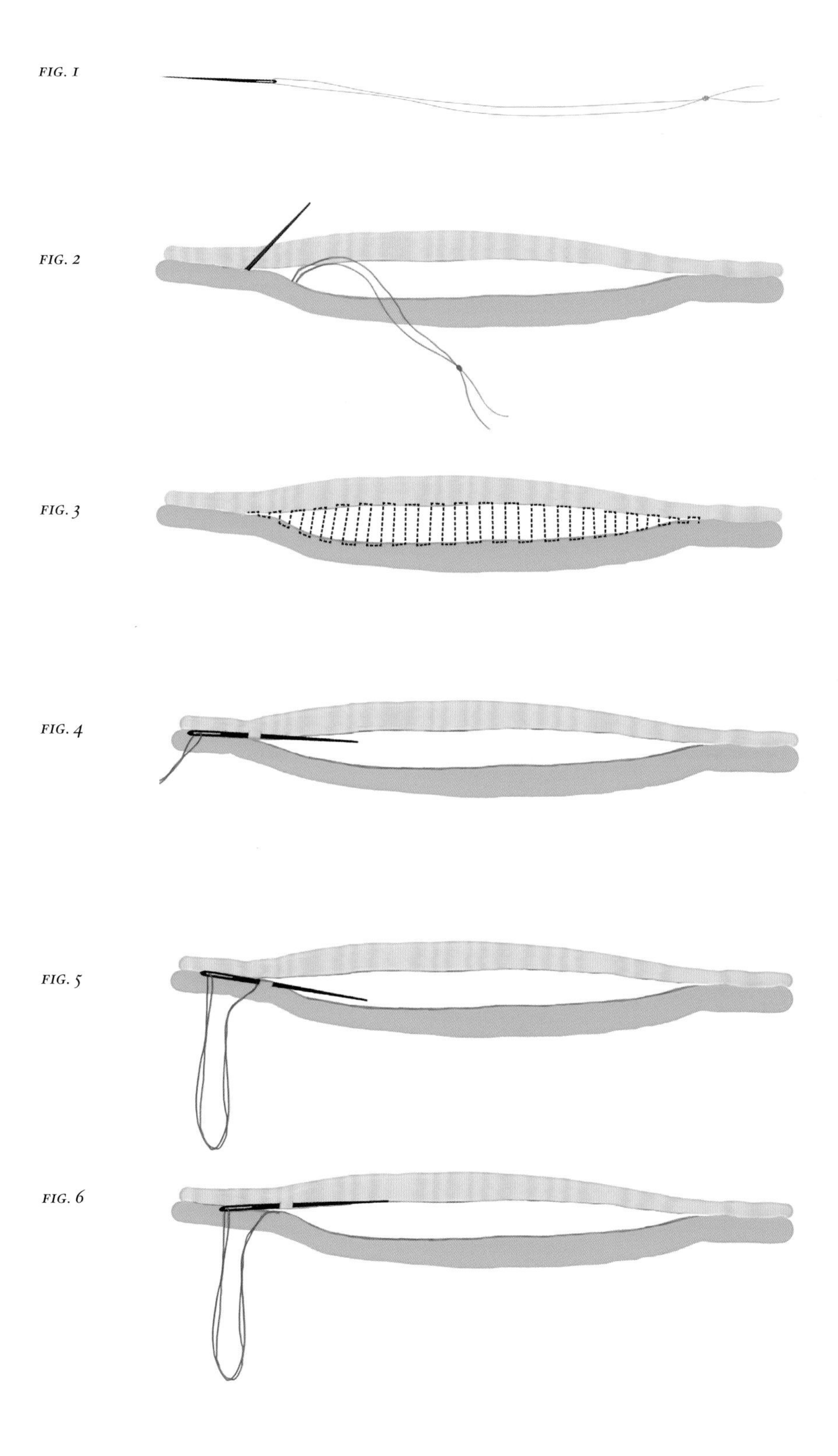
FIG. 1
FIG. 2
FIG. 3
FIG. 4
FIG. 5
FIG. 6

Gift Card Elephant Softie

These templates have been reduced in size to fit this book. Enlarge templates at 200% for correct project scale.

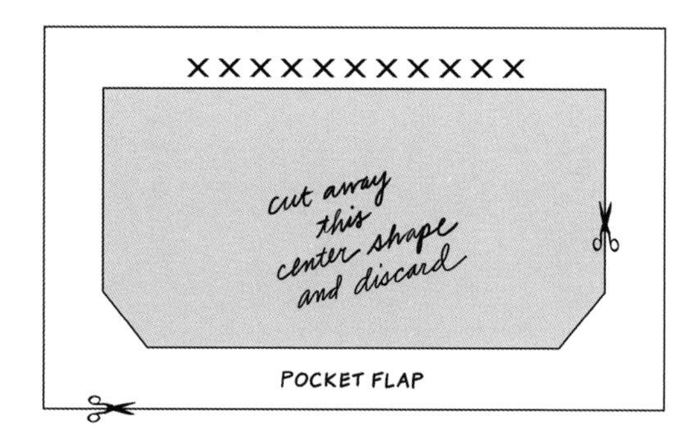

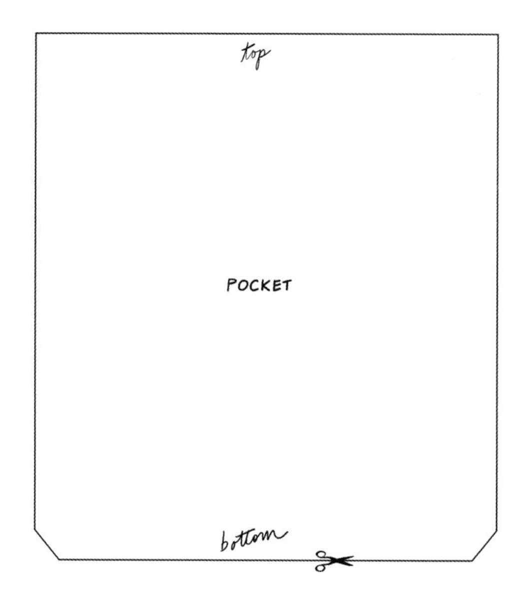

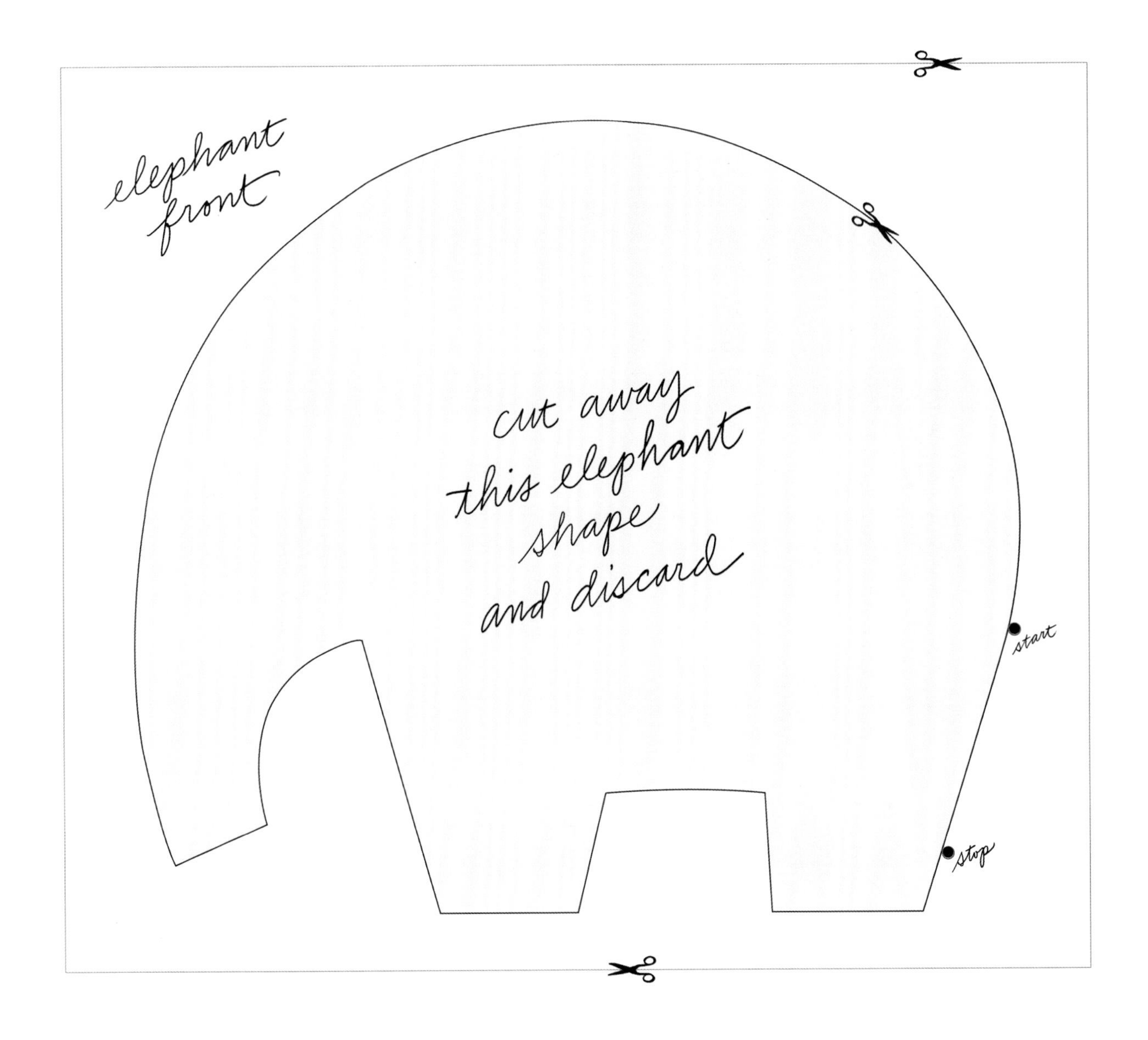
elephant front
cut away this elephant shape and discard
start
stop

Gift Card Truck Softie

These templates have been reduced in size to fit this book.
Enlarge templates at 200% for correct project scale.

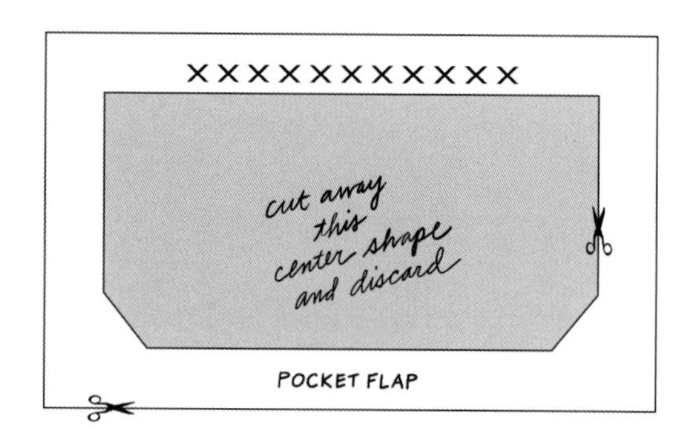

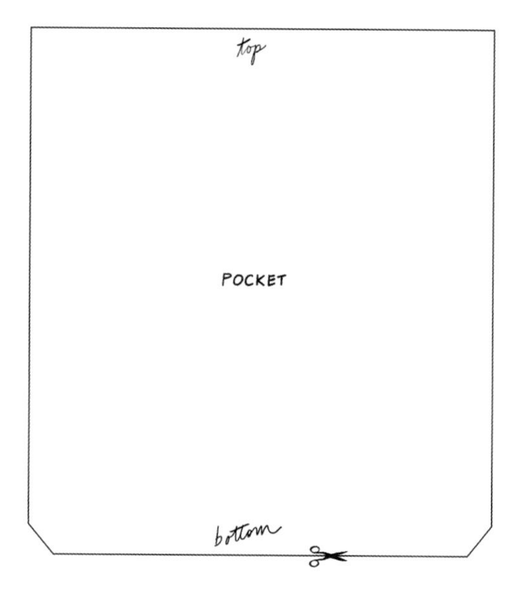

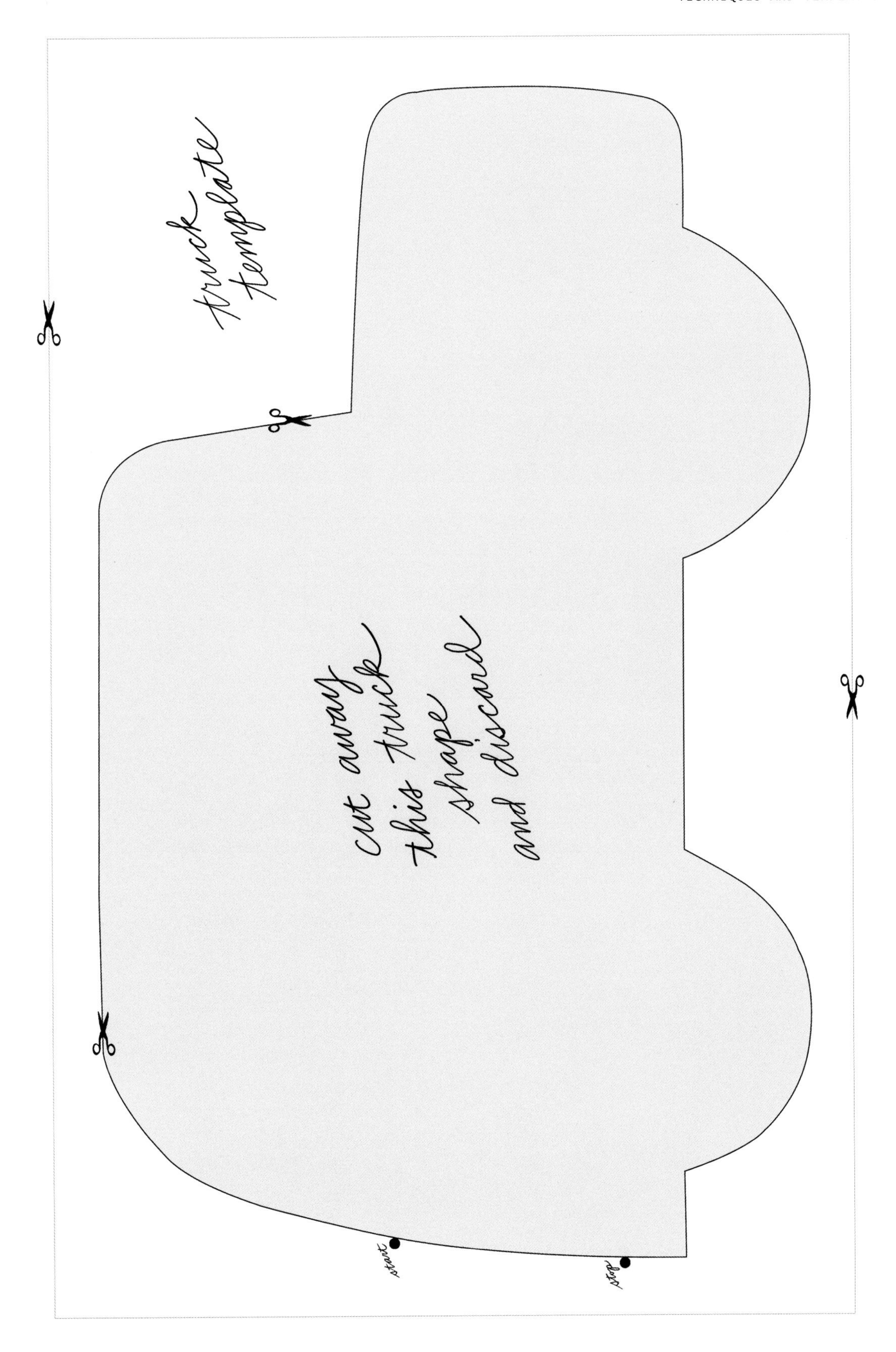
truck template
cut away this truck shape and discard
start
stop

Ruby Star's Chinese Takeout Box

This template has been reduced in size to fit this book. Enlarge template at 200% for correct project scale.

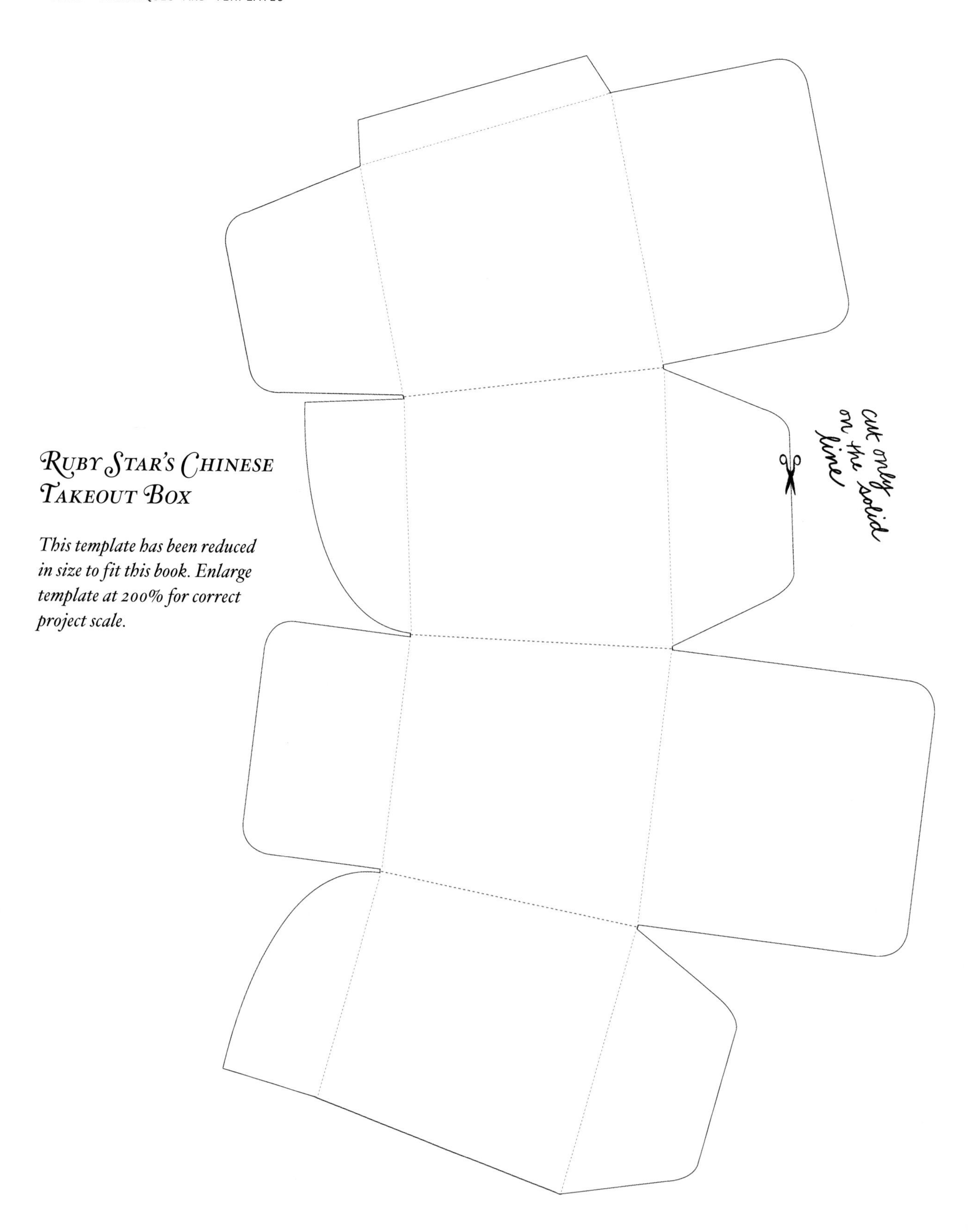
cut only on the solid line

Newspaper Flower

This template is shown actual size.

ACKNOWLEDGMENTS

Because we live with them, we have to begin by thanking our husbands. Without Gregory Miller's photography and Blake Tannery's art direction, this book could never have turned out so beautifully. We do love you and appreciate you.

We should, and want to, praise Atlanta's indomitable Deborah Moebes, of the amazing sewing lounge Whipstitch, and the book *Stitch by Stitch* (which I actually used to learn to sew). Deborah has been Melody's, and therefore my, champion from the very beginning. The summer of 2010, she introduced Melody to Ellen Luckett Baker, author of *1, 2, 3 Sew*, who remains a dear, encouraging, and supportive friend. Ellen was pivotal in our getting this book published. Upon our first meeting, she said, "Here! You should call my agent, she'd love you guys!"

Kate McKean, with Howard Morhaim Literary Agency, treated us like long-lost best friends. She was immediately enthusiastic and told us she believed in our little idea. We specifically remember she told us it was a bit unusual, but *someone* would want it. We'd find that someone.

So that leads us to our serene editor, Jennifer Urban-Brown, of Roost Books. We must thank her for loving our idea just the way she saw it, the first time. And for leading us to believe we really could, actually in real life, write a book. While Melody and I were full of questions during our first call together, she was all, "Cool, it's all good. You know what you're doing." It felt a bit like being told it was time to take the new baby home from the hospital. We were sort of panicky, but Jennifer's confidence calmed us.

We also get to thank the wonderful, influential Kristin Link, of the wildly popular blog *Sew, Mama, Sew!* (http://sewmamasew.com). In December of 2010, she collaborated with The Green Bag Lady to host *The Green Grocery Bag Challenge,* and we were amazed to see how many of her readers were as excited by reusable gift packaging as we were. On a whim, we asked her to contribute to our book. Without much prior knowledge of us, but with an appreciation of Melody's fabric and a brief meeting at the Houston Quilt Market, she agreed to write our foreword. We felt we'd struck gold. We still do. She is one of many in this community who help to make us feel we belong.

And then? Then?!? On a lark, one Saturday morning last summer, Melody, Greg, Blake, and I got the ridiculously improbable idea to email Elsie Larson, of the amazing blog *A Beautiful Mess* (http://abeautifulmess.typepad.com) and the unbelievable Red Velvet Shop. We wanted to see if we could strike a deal to do part of our book's photo shoot in her Springfield, Missouri, store. Although we'd never had any contact with her before, she loved our little project-that-could and agreed to let us come on out! Her space with our stuff was a great collaboration, and she, with new husband Jeremy, served as models when we needed to add a bit of life to the projects. Thank you, thank you, thank you to Elsie, Jeremy, and sister, Emma Chapman, who helped coordinate all the communication and details. And besides the great vintage wear, home items, amazing space, gracious hearts . . . yum! They sell sweets, too! There is an entire case of cupcakes. But even more? Elsie sent me home with a mid-century media cart,

which is three shelves on a chrome frame with wheels, painted red. I asked what she'd take for it, and she just gave it to me. I'd been looking for one for months, and now I have this fabulous memory of the trip to the Red Velvet Shop, right in my kitchen. Thank you again, Elsie, Jeremy, and Emma.

Ross Martin (http://rossmartinphotography.com) must be recognized. He is his own one-man photo shop but often assists Greg Miller. He came out to the Red Velvet Shop with us and made what would have been a really grueling trip—running up and down several floors of a hundred-year-old brick-front mercantile with all the equipment—a very pleasant, dare we even say fun, one. OK. Maybe not *fun*. But he brought the Rossome. Thanks so much, Ross.

Acknowledging these people surely doesn't cover a fraction of the divine individuals who have lent hands and hearts to help us. Fellow designers and crafters we love, bloggers who support us, sewists who have shared their time and talents with us . . . just-plain-lovely people who have taken a few minutes or more to give us their warmth and encouragement and to share their creativity. We couldn't be more grateful. Thank you all.

Last, but with big emphasis on not being least, we are thrilled to thank our project testers. These ladies made the difference in our *thinking and hoping* we'd provided good, clear instructions, and our feeling confident that we have. Their feedback gave us renewed enthusiasm, encouragement, and critical insight. When we'd gone over and over and over a pattern, and couldn't possibly add another anything, they not only saw something that may need clarification but in many cases, had fun, different ways to approach the projects and reuse them later. Sincerest thanks to:

Brittney Anderson, *Brittney Anderson,*
http://brittneyanderson.blogspot.com

Katherine Skene, *Carolyn and Me,*
http://carolyn-and-me.blogspot.com

Rachel Locke, *Sweet Tea Mom,*
http://sweetteamom.blogspot.com

Jen Carlton Bailey, or affectionately, *Betty Crocker Ass,* the blog, www.bettycrockerass.com

Megan Bohr, *Canoe Ridge Creations,*
www.canoeridgecreations.com

Jeanne Gwin, *The Learning Curve,*
http://jeannegwin.blogspot.com

Jenni Alexander, of the etsy shop jenni20,
www.etsy.com/shop/jenni20

Everyone always says it, but this writing a book thing is *quite* a journey. We can't tell those of you who helped make it a reality thank you enough. Including our folks, who volunteered for the very unglamorous job of keeping children many, many nights and weekends when time was tight and tensions were riding high. We love you. You saved your grandchildren's lives.

ABOUT THE AUTHORS

Melody Miller

Once upon a time, Melody had a secret alter ego. In her fantasies, she was Ruby Star, and she achieved great, creative things. And then, in real life, she really did. With a background in fine art, Melody has done everything from study industrial design to work as a makeup artist and, later, as a graphic designer and marketing maven. After the birth of her second child, she decided to stay home and start her own business sewing custom window panels. Shortly thereafter, she taught herself to sew.

Everyone who meets her loves her huge doe eyes and gigantic heart. They also love her work. Her first line of fabric, Ruby Star Rising for Kokka, was released in the fall of 2010 with great reception. Melody lives in Atlanta, Georgia, not quite close enough to Allison, in picturesque and historic Grant Park with her amazing photographer hubby, two charmingly quirky children, and a somewhat simple-minded Bichon Frise. Without Melody, Allison has nothing about which to write. While Melody prefers to send her kids to a lovely school, she thinks Allison is brave for keeping all her kids home every day. She loves vintage design, flea markets, her converse sneaks (in metallic bronze), and margaritas. Most times, in moderation. Check her out at www.melodymiller.net.

Allison Tannery

Several years ago, Allison knew nothing about sewing except to consider her machine a mortal enemy, and nothing about gift wrapping outside of store-bought paper and stick-on bows. There had been the newspaper funnies her grandmother used back in the day to wrap the likes of McDonald's Looney Tunes collector glasses, but then again, Grandma was mostly being cheap. Allison studied journalism at The University of Georgia, but that career track lost its luster when she fell in love with a long-haired musician/artist and promptly had four children. She never got over wanting to write.

Allison lives just outside of Atlanta, Georgia, with those four children, husband of nearly twenty years (who has since cut his hair short), and one incredibly annoying dog. She is the Brand Champion—the personal cheerleader for Melody Miller's work, her PR Rep, and the one who keeps the calendars and writes the emails. She is now also, very gratefully, a budding author. While she once baked wedding cakes for a living, she now only does box cakes for her own children's birthdays. Without Allison, Melody would have no one to make fun of and no one with whom she can solve the world's problems. In her spare time, Allison homeschools the children, watches reruns of *Law and Order,* and drinks copious amounts of house chardonnay. Check her out at www.allisontannery.com.

ANSWER